RONNIE DREW

Ronnie

PENGUIN
IRELAND

PENGUIN IRELAND

Published by the Penguin Group
Penguin Ireland, 25 St Stephen's Green, Dublin 2, Ireland
(a division of Penguin Books Ltd)
Penguin Books Ltd, 80 Strand, London WC2R 0RL, England
Penguin Group (USA) Inc., 375 Hudson Street, New York, New York 10014, USA
Penguin Group (Australia), 250 Camberwell Road, Camberwell, Victoria 3124, Australia
(a division of Pearson Australia Group Pty Ltd)
Penguin Group (Canada), 90 Eglinton Avenue East, Suite 700, Toronto, Ontario, Canada M4P 2Y3
(a division of Pearson Penguin Canada Inc.)
Penguin Books India Pvt Ltd, 11 Community Centre, Panchsheel Park, New Delhi – 110 017, India
Penguin Group (NZ), 67 Apollo Drive, Rosedale, North Shore 0632, New Zealand
(a division of Pearson New Zealand Ltd)
Penguin Books (South Africa) (Pty) Ltd, 24 Sturdee Avenue,
Rosebank, Johannesburg 2196, South Africa

Penguin Books Ltd, Registered Offices: 80 Strand, London WC2R 0RL, England

www.penguin.com

First published 2008
1

Copyright © Cliodhna Dunne and Phelim Drew, 2008

The moral right of the author has been asserted

The Acknowledgements on pages 292–4 constitute an extension of this copyright page

Set in 10.5/14 pt Postscript Linotype Sabon
Typeset by Rowland Phototypesetting Ltd, Bury St Edmunds, Suffolk
Printed in Great Britain by Clays Ltd, St Ives plc

A CIP catalogue record for this book is available from the British Library

ISBN: 978-1-844-88198-7

www.greenpenguin.co.uk

Penguin Books is committed to a sustainable future
for our business, our readers and our planet.
The book in your hands is made from paper
certified by the Forest Stewardship Council.

In memory of Deirdre Drew

And for Ruaidhrí, Aoife, Vivian, Milo, Seánie and Lily

One afternoon, as we were walking along the banks of that wonderful Seville River, we sat down on an old bench, because Ronnie said he wanted to tell me something serious about himself and music. I said fair enough. Anyway, to make a long story short, he simply told me that he wanted to be a ballad singer and what did I think about the idea? I said that truly I didn't know because I'd never heard him sing (he was taking flamenco guitar classes at the time).

'Sing me a bar or two of some ballad, Ronnie,' I said, 'and I'll give you my honest opinion for what it's worth.' So there and then he set out on that lovely song, 'Nora'.

Well, he sang it in such an unusual way, with great feeling, and in that raspy voice of his (as you well know!) that I was immediately convinced and advised him to forget the flamenco and head back for Dublin. He took the train to Madrid the following day, and on to Dublin.

And that's the gospel. Fine things, like falling in love, etc., usually happen in the simplest of ways, i.e. uncomplicated and straightforward. And your dad, God bless, like Lot's wife, never looked back.

Letter from Joe Hackett to Cliodhna Dunne
La Carihuela, Spain, September 2008

Contents

Preface

Some of my warmest memories of my father involve the long walks, or 'drives', that my sister and I would take with him when we were children. My mother was always absent from these excursions, not being the walking or driving-the-country type. She was more the smoking, chatting and drinking-tea-in-the-kitchen type. I think she saw these trips as an opportunity to get us all out of the house.

We would drive around Wicklow, often visiting the same places, the familiarity proving a source of comfort. I can confidently say that I don't look back on these memories with rose-tinted glasses: there was a genuine warmth and ease on these journeys. Like a lot of performers my dad found it difficult to adjust to normality between tours, but these outings afforded him the opportunity to truly unwind, without actually doing nothing.

The period between 1975 and 1980, when he had left The Dubliners to make a go of it as a solo artist, was the most difficult for him and a hugely challenging time. The popularity of live acts in the pubs and clubs of Ireland had begun to wane, giving way to other forms of entertainment and presenting problems professionally and therefore financially. Thankfully the option of going back to The Dubliners was there, and Dad continued to tour with Barney, John, Eamonn and Seán for years, enjoying many successes.

Throughout all this, during the short breaks between tours, our walks and drives continued. As his many friends and admirers will testify, when in a relaxed frame of mind he could be the most engaging person you could hope to meet, interesting and at times deadly serious, but always with a rich and mischievous sense of humour. The many hours we spent in this way were reassuringly intimate but also extremely entertaining – moments when I could selfishly indulge in having my father to myself. One thing that I remember, and that stands out about our drives, was that he always took pleasure in taking a road that we had never been on to see what it might throw up and, more importantly for him, to see where we would come out. Needless to say, I think this reflected his character: intensely curious, courageous in going his own way and fearless in being himself.

In later years he was to find an inner peace that up till then had seemed to elude him. This gave him the strength to leave The Dubliners again, to leave the big tours behind, but this time his reasons were much clearer and his aspirations more attainable. He toured for years at his own pace in a successful one-man show supported by Mike Hanrahan. It was around this time that, unfortunately for me, he took up golf – another progression that confounded those closest to him. This occupation, which replaced our trips, gave him a huge amount of satisfaction. He revelled in the personal challenge of the game, enjoyed its social side and always liked being surrounded by nature.

I will cherish the memory of our time spent together walking in Glendalough or travelling the back roads of Wicklow. I am sorry now that I didn't record his many stories, recollections and observations but then again there are some things that are not meant to be recorded. He lived for the here and now, for good and bad, through ups and downs. It was this quality that I think led him to be a performer, gaining satisfaction from communicating with people, whether through humorous anecdotes, biting satire or socially and politically conscious ballads.

He was in every respect at the centre of our family, and his loss is something I'm not sure we will ever come to terms with; we will merely have to learn to live with it.

I hope you take some of the pleasure that I enjoyed with my father while reading his words, as well as the contributions of his friends, and perusing the photographs that I hope provide an insight into his private life.

Special thanks to Patricia Deevy and Michael McLoughlin from Penguin Ireland in following through with this book and for their hard work and sensitivity. Many thanks also to the many people who have helped and supported us in ways too numerous to mention.

Phelim Drew, October 2008

PART I

In his own words

My father, Ronnie, abhorred sentimentality and favoured honesty. The songs he chose to sing were always very honest, telling their story in a poetic way but without any unnecessary frills. He never undertook anything lightly, and when he came across a song he loved he needed to spend quite a long time learning it. It was very important to him to understand absolutely the song, its words, its story and its music. During this learning period he would decide how to interpret the song and ultimately perform it.

Dad had a fantastic memory for dates and facts. He loved good stories, both written and oral, and was always on the lookout for a good yarn, and the manner in which they were written or told was very important. When he decided to undertake the writing of his autobiography, he approached it in his usual manner and gave each story a lot of thought and time before committing it to paper. Unfortunately, his illness cut the autobiography short and we will never get to read all the rich stories of a man who loved life, always lived it to the full and never took a moment for granted.

He wrote as he spoke, and this to my mind gives each of his stories a great charm. Once again, his need for honesty and distaste for sentimentality shine through.

Cliodhna Dunne, October 2008

Chapter 1

I don't know for sure, but I presume I was born at home and that was in a big house in Glasthule, which is about a mile from Dún Laoghaire, and eight miles south of Dublin.

We didn't of course own the house, but, from the bits and pieces of information I picked up along the way, I gathered that after their marriage my mother and father rented a flat in it while they waited to move into a new house in Monkstown Farm, an old farm on which dwelling places for the working-class people of Dún Laoghaire and surrounding areas were being built.

I remember moving into this new house, No. 37 Oliver Plunkett Avenue. These houses were extremely well built, consisting of three bedrooms, a kitchen, a sitting room, a bathroom and a garden, front and back. I have one isolated memory of this time. Mr Smith, our next-door neighbour, was digging his garden, so I came out to watch him and he put on a show for me: he stopped digging, reached down and picked up a worm, threw his head back and opening his mouth wide dropped the worm from his upstretched hand into, as I thought, his open mouth. I did not feel squeamish, just amazed.

Shortly after we moved into the new house, I found myself living in my maternal grandparents' house in Dún Laoghaire. I don't recall the move; I just remember that I was now living there. My brother Gerry, who was three years younger than me, must have come along just about then, and presumably I was sent to my grandparents to be minded while my mother gave birth, and afterwards it seems I just continued living there. This was not so strange as it might appear today; I was later to find out that quite a few boys had also been brought up by their grannies and it was not looked upon

3

as being anything worthy of serious comment one way or another.

My grandfather won some money, I don't know how much, in the national sweep, sometime in the late thirties or early forties. In those days the top prize was £25,000. He didn't win that much, but what he did win went towards building a house. With his own background being a carpenter, he built the house himself, a detached house on Tivoli Terrace. That added another bit of poshness to it.

My grandfather was a sober, kind, hard-working man, whom I don't remember saying very much. In any case, in those days the bringing-up of young children was the prerogative of the women in the family and I was more or less brought up by my grandmother (known to me as Nanny) and my three aunts, Eileen, May and Lal. This state of affairs was to lead to very unsettling consequences for myself and all those who were involved with me.

Being brought up by four women is definitely not to be recommended, not that the results of it were any fault of theirs or mine. I was to become a very selfish child, though I didn't recognize it as that; it was just that in my situation I took it for granted that things were done for me and I accepted these things without question. I was, in effect, a spoiled brat. As year followed year I was to become nothing less than a little bollix, who accepted kindnesses and whatever treats were offered to me without any real thankfulness.

When I eventually went to school it was to an infant school, which was in an orphanage, run by an order of nuns who, strangely in those days, wore civilian clothes and were called Miss. My only memory of that time is of a teacher called Miss Keegan.

My entry into the real world was to take place when I was sent to the Christian Brothers School in Dún Laoghaire. Now I was not at all prepared for this, because up to that time I had never had to make any kind of effort to do anything for myself, and so I just didn't even try.

My first experience of the world on emerging from the cocoon in which I had existed was not pleasant, and was probably the birth of the low self-esteem which plagued me for many years and, if I were to dwell upon it, probably still does.

I was dreadful at the 'sums' and the punishment for this was not a beating, despite the reputation that the Christian Brothers have had for that kind of thing. Halfway through the morning the entire class was taken out to the schoolyard for exercise, which consisted of us being marched around for, I suppose, fifteen minutes. For all this period I was made to carry a ball frame (an abacus) to advertise, publicly as it were, my stupidity. I don't remember what I thought about it at the time, but I remember it vividly, as it was probably my first experience of feeling inferior. I was not bright enough, nor courageous enough, nor had I enough spirit to castigate myself and to say, 'I'll fight this,' and to put my mind to learning sums. I had never had to fight for anything before, so I just wanted to get out of there and back to my sheltered existence.

Things did not improve, because when I was about seven we had a visit from the public health doctor to our school, during which the pupils were medically examined. I was to find out after that I had 'tonsils and adenoids' which would have to be surgically removed. The outward signs of this condition were not designed to make you any more attractive and I had obviously had it for some time before it was diagnosed. The main visible symptom was an open mouth, and I had an open mouth which had earned me the nickname 'Gawky'. I didn't know what it meant, but, taken with my other nickname, 'Saucer Eyes', and the ball-frame incident, and the taunts that followed me having to march around the schoolyard with it, I realized that not alone was I stupid but I was ugly into the bargain. Now all this had a devastating effect on me. I made no friends at school and at a very young age was essentially a loner.

Shortly after being diagnosed with the tonsils and adenoids I was brought to get them out, probably by some of my aunts. Memory only supplies me with a segment of my experience in hospital. I remember seeing a railed affair around the cot in which I had been placed. The next thing I remember was being awakened by what must have been a nurse, who took me by the hand and brought me to a white tiled room. She put me sitting on a bench and left. I studied the striped pyjamas I was wearing and I now realize this was the first time in my life that I felt loneliness, fear and desolation. A trolley arrived to interrupt my musings, and I was wheeled into another white tiled room which was much brighter. Then a nurse placed a mask over my nose and face. To this day, even when I read the word 'ether' I get that smell.

Chapter 2

My grandfather was an abstemious and very meticulous man. He had begun his working life as a carpenter, but by the time I had gone to live in his house he was some class of an inspector with Dún Laoghaire Corporation, something to do with concrete. I understood that he checked footpaths that had been newly constructed, to make sure that they were fit to be walked on by the citizens of the borough of Dún Laoghaire.

This job carried with it a certain respectability, for he did not have to wear overalls. He also enjoyed a couple of great perks: every year he was told to go to a certain tailor and to have himself measured for a three-piece blue serge suit, which included a spare pair of trousers. This was at a time when even official organizations like the Dún Laoghaire Corporation had a modicum of taste, and the suits were never marred by logos or badges, which meant he could wear these clothes outside of working hours without feeling conspicuous.

He was also issued with a three-speed Raleigh bicycle. Now the bikes were not thrown out with such frequency as the suits. The bike was replaced only when it had gone beyond repair. One of the requisites for a man riding a bicycle in those days was a pair of bicycle clips. These were sprung metal affairs with a gap in each one, allowing them to be placed around the trouser ends at the ankle, thus preventing the trousers from becoming entangled in the bike's mechanism. Slovenly folk might pull their socks up over the ends of their trousers, but my grandfather was no sloven. In fact he made his own clips – two pieces of very thin steel wire with the ends bent into hooks. They were only about two inches long, and when he dismounted immediately he fished a small neat stainless-steel container out of a waistcoat pocket into which he put them for safe keeping. He also made his own pens from bits and pieces of broken pens – I still have one of them. He was a man ahead of his time, with a strong belief that nothing should be bought that could be made from bits and pieces which were lying about. Recycling, you might say.

Now this finicky behaviour was to have consequences for me. From the age of about eleven up until my early twenties I spent a lot of time living in hope that I would at sometime get the 'real thing'. For example, that I might get 'real' socks, because the ones knitted by my granny were different to everyone else's – even at that time younger mothers had given up knitting socks.

I was never, nor was I ever to become, a sporty or athletic type, but as a young lad of eleven or twelve years of age I was madly trying to fit in, and was trying to get involved in the games that most of the young fellows around about were playing. For one of my first forays into sportsmanship, I decided I would try hurling. I mentioned this in a casual way to the household in general, hoping that a broad hint might result in an offer to buy me a hurley. Alas, my grandfather interjected to say that such a purchase would be a waste of money and that he would make me the best hurley in Ireland. My heart nearly failed me, because somewhere deep down I knew that even though he would probably be capable of making me a very good one, I also knew that it would be somehow different.

And so it turned out. He trotted off to the library and came back with an illustrated history of hurling and he took his model from a drawing of a hurley as used by Fionn Mac Cumhaill or someone from the very distant past. It bore only a passing resemblance to the hurleys then in use. My grandfather, as if to prove that he was as ignorant about the sport as I was, made the hurley out of teak or mahogany, not understanding that hurleys are traditionally made of ash, so that the finished article has a springy feel to it when the ball is struck. His hurley was heavy and rigid and utterly useless for the game of hurling.

Under his watchful eye I more or less insinuated myself into a game that was being played in the street. When I eventually managed to get a whack at the ball, I got a jarring shock, and felt like I might dislocate a shoulder. I could probably have dealt with this, but my fellow hurlers laughed and pointed at my hurley. This was too much for me: I never tried to play the game again.

The sad look on my grandfather's face told of his disappointment in his grandson's inability to persevere and make a stand of some sort. He was probably right.

Shortly after the hurley-stick affair he made me a scimitar, no less. It was a lovely piece of work, made from a light plywood, which was all smoothed and sandpapered. I could hardly wait to get into the street where the boys in the neighbourhood were playing 'sword fighting'. I looked forward to them envying my special sword. Sure what had they, God help them? Only a long piece of old stick onto which was nailed or tied a shorter piece of a lath as the crosspiece. Very shabby-looking, I decided.

Of course, the opposite was the case. As soon as I entered the fray, the obvious finger-pointing and vocal derision of my scimitar had the effect of causing me once more to quail and to slink off with my tail between my legs. I put my sword in what was called the garage (a structure at the side of the house whose name had always puzzled me because it had never housed a car; it was home to all kinds of cast-off bric-a-brac, and there was a workbench under the window, much used by the maker of hurleys, swords, etc.).

Having left my sword with all the other redundancies, I began to feel sad, not only for myself but also for Da, as he was known within the family, because he was obviously a kindly, well-meaning man and I felt I had once again let him down.

Da was also a great man for living as though he had to keep to some sort of timetable, though it was a timetable he had set himself. Around the corner from where we lived was the convent of the Little Sisters of the Poor, and every morning at seven o'clock he would hear Mass in their small chapel. Not wishing to cast any doubt on his piety, I always felt he harboured a certain amount of innocent pride in this daily activity. While there were no actual rules or regulations on who could attend Mass at the nuns' place, it was generally accepted in the neighbourhood that only those people who had helped to ease their worldly lot by carrying out certain tasks for them should do so. At one time, wearing his carpenter's hat, Da had installed a wooden altar rail in their small chapel, which of course had been a labour of love, and this more or less entitled him to his place on the secular side of the same altar rail. After Mass he would return home, have his breakfast and be at his work before eight thirty.

Every evening, usually at the same time, and with some ceremony, he would give out the rosary. Da would place his elbows on the table, while my grandmother, my three aunts and myself would kneel with our elbows on the kitchen chairs. When this prayer had finished, that was only the half of it, because then we had the 'trimmings', which consisted of three Hail Marys for all deceased relations, three Hail Marys 'for the sailors', three Hail Marys for 'those without a roof over their heads', and so on and so on.

Da's week's toil ended as far as I remember at 12.30 on Saturday, when he would come home, change from his working blue suit into his good blue suit and head for the bookies. His weekend off had begun and he would spend the afternoon doing one shilling doubles, trebles, accumulators and other combinations which the family referred to, with a modicum of sarcasm, as 'Da's one shilling miracles'.

When his lust for gambling had been satisfied until the following week, he would return home for his tea, and when this was finished he would read the paper and listen to the news on the radio.

Then, with the air of a man who felt that he had been lazing around for long enough and it was time for him to carry out some more serious duties, he would rise from his chair and announce that he had to do some of his chores, one of which I remember was polishing, with almost militant zeal, his own and my grandmother's shoes in readiness for Sunday. When this task had been completed he would set off for the Workmen's Club to have a game of cards. He had at one time been the manager of this club. He had also been the captain of Dún Laoghaire fire brigade, had played the coronet in the Erin's Own brass band, and more besides. But these are stories for another day.

Da was the master in his own house, which, in these enlightened and politically correct days, may seem to be a very archaic notion, but there you have it: that was the status quo at the time and did not seem at all strange.

In the arena of proving himself to be the head of the household, he pulled off what I have always considered to be his master stroke. There was in existence in those days the social convention of inviting people 'to tea'. Dinner, which was usually partaken of in the middle of the day, was a familial affair and it would have been regarded as not the thing to have it overlooked by comparative strangers, and so it was not a runner in the invitational stakes. Lunch was what a man took to work and consisted mainly of some kind of sandwiches wrapped up in paper.

This tea business was not quite as simple as it might appear. Depending on the perceived importance, or lack of it, of the invitees, it could be a very simple affair consisting of tea and cake, of tea, sandwiches and cake, or a full blown fry-up of rashers, sausages, eggs and maybe even toast, and this would be followed by tea and cake.

My mother's sister Eileen was an unmarried lady and was employed as a tailoress/cutter in an establishment that specialized in the making of ladies' clothes. Due to her being a tradeswoman she was more or less in charge in the workroom, the area in which the actual clothes were made and finished. One day she put it to my grandmother that she felt she would like to invite three of her lady colleagues to tea. Nanny said that they would be very welcome, as she was sure that they were 'very nice respectable young women, and sure why wouldn't they be, and they working in that nice place owned by Mr Connolly, who everybody knows is a gentleman to his fingertips'.

As the date of the girls' visit drew near, while sitting around the fire my aunts Eileen, May and Lal went into conclave with 'Mother' about an important issue which could very possibly mar, or at least cast a shadow on, the forthcoming event, and that this issue concerned 'Father'.

Now, part of Da's apparel, along with his three-piece blue serge suit, was what was called in those days an Anthony Eden hat. I was to discover years later that its official description was a Homburg hat. Most men at that time wore headgear of some sort: it could have been a cap, a felt hat, a fedora, a trilby or even an Anthony Eden.

So what about it? You might ask.

Well, there was this about it: Da's hat left his head only when he said the rosary, went to Mass or went to bed. At all other times the hat remained on what he considered its rightful place – his head. When he was out and about the hat was pulled low on his forehead, and when he came into his own house it was shoved up from the forehead and rested on the back of his head and it remained in this position while he was indoors, which included mealtimes. I need hardly say that due to all the pushing and shoving the hat had a somewhat battered appearance.

This was the important issue at the centre of the confab between my aunts and my grandmother. Aunt Eileen and Aunt May were pointing out to Mother that these girls who were coming to tea were very respectable and came of decent people and would be shocked and maybe even scandalized at the very idea of Father wearing his hat, and a battered old hat into the bargain, while he ate his tea. Mother agreed that such a thing could well cast a slur on the family from which it might never recover, and indeed we could be the talk of the town, and that she would have a word with him.

The day of the tea finally arrived and with it the three girls, who on arrival were introduced with much ceremony to 'Mother', 'Father' (hat still in place), Aunt May and Aunt Lal. The ladies were seated around the table when Da, who had been outside, came in – bareheaded – and took his place at the head of the table. The meal was served and it was of the rasher-and-egg variety. It was a convivial repast and the ladies had a great chat.

Da remained silent, except when asked a direct question. All in all he seldom had much conversation with women. From certain remarks I had overheard him drop into conversation with other men, I worked out that he considered that because women did not discuss politics, racing or football, but only chatted about style, the price of children's shoes and the cost of various food items and other mundane topics, it was as well to let them at it and not to interfere.

The tea was turning out a great success, Aunt Eileen's friends proving themselves to be ladies in the extreme, as they complimented the lady of the house on the freshness of the eggs, the superior quality of the bacon, etc. They had just started on the cake when Da rattled the room with a sneeze. There was a pause. Without a word, he rose from the table, left the room for about thirty seconds, returned and took his place again, this time with his hat on the back of his head.

Chapter 3

My grandmother, as I remember, seldom went out, except of course to attend Mass, or some of the other pious practices that were very much on the go in those days. There was Benediction, an evening devotion which consisted of a recital of the rosary, prayers for those who had fallen away from the practice of their religion (the Catholic religion, of course), prayers for the conversion of Russia, prayers for peace in whatever part of the world the worst war was going on in, and so on and so on.

During Benediction two altar boys were in attendance, one of them in charge of the thurible, a piece of equipment that hung from his hand on fine silver chains. These chains were attached to a silver sphere that was divided into two halves and had also in its make-up a series of elaborate air holes of an ecclesiastically inspired design. The thurible contained reddened (burning) charcoal. To keep the charcoal alight the altar boy had to swing the thurible from side to side by its chains, which most did with great gusto.

The second altar boy held what was called an incense boat. This looked for all the world like an ornate silver sauceboat complete with a small ladle-like spoon. At a certain point in the proceedings the young fella in charge of the thurible would raise the top half of the sphere, thus exposing the reddened charcoal. The priest would then be offered 'the boat' by the other lad and from this he would ladle incense onto the burning coal, instantly creating great plumes of aromatic smoke. Mix this with the scent of burning wax candles and in a very short time an odour of sanctity pervaded the whole chapel. And to add to the holy atmosphere, there was hymn-singing.

The ceremony ended by the priest holding a magnificent golden monstrance high above his head. The centrepiece of this was the sacred host and emanating from the host was a series of long fluted gold strips representing, I imagine, the rays of the sun. These formed a kind of irregular circle of about two and a half feet in diameter. I once heard Nanny saying as she returned from Benediction, 'It was like heaven in that chapel tonight.'

St Michael's Church in Dún Laoghaire was our parish church, but it was not much patronized by my grandmother. For her, I think (though she would never have given tongue to such a thought), there was a certain commonness about St Michael's. How much nicer and more sedate it was to attend Mass at the chapel of the Little Sisters of the Poor, or evening devotions at the chapel of the nuns who ran St Joseph's Orphanage. I mean, you wouldn't find the 'riff-raff' carrying out their religious duties in the chapels of the nuns.

I don't, and never have, blamed my grandmother for her modest aspirations in the area of social-climbing, as it is now called. It was not her idea to reach the top of the social ladder, but to rise by two or three rungs would do no harm and would prove that she had 'got on' in the world – on the face of it, not asking for a lot.

My grandparents would have been Fine Gael, and Fine Gael was kind of a posh party at the time. The Fine Gaelers were up the ladder a bit, not like Fianna Fáil; they were all ruffians and republicans. In Dún Laoghaire they used to say things about people, 'oh, they're too Irish' or 'they're terrible Irish', meaning they were extremely low. What they meant was, like, it was over-the-top Irish, a bit too green. Their main desire was to be posh or to move up the social ladder a bit. Their aspirations were very mild and I was picked on to be the saviour. As long as I got a job where I was wearing a suit, it didn't really matter about the money part.

My grandmother and grandfather, and all my aunts, while they were Catholics, were aware that Protestants were, in general, more polite people and nice people and they had a good thrift ethos. They wanted to have that too. My aunts used to try to emulate this, but they got so mean then; they wouldn't put coal on the fire and you'd be freezing.

Along with all this Nanny practised a kind of petty snobbery, which was to have a bad effect on me for many years. This was not because it caused me any great psychological damage – or maybe it did, and I haven't recognized it – but one of the effects of living with all this was that I became very confused. I could not understand how a person professing to be a Christian could not seem to understand the concept of charity except in a one-dimensional way, like giving a couple of pence to a poor man or woman. And I could not understand how you could be selective with regard to the meaning of the Sermon on the Mount, or that stealing could only be said to be carried out if it was with the help of a gun and with a mask over your face.

My grandmother was not the only person who adopted this one-dimensional attitude to Christianity. It was par for the course, being practised all around me. Is it any wonder I was confused?

Despite her adherence to Catholicism, I don't think my grandmother knew or cared very much what its real tenets might be. 'Whatever the priest tells ye offa the altar should be good enough for ye, instead of askin' questions the pope couldn't answer and talking about the Bible. Sure, everybody knows that it's a mortal sin to read the Bible . . . In any case, only Protestants read the Bible.'

She more or less gave in that Protestants were Christians of a sort, but whenever this had to be acknowledged it was done grudgingly and you could hear the doubt in her voice. It wasn't that she was a bigot, she just did not seem to comprehend that Protestants and Catholics shared more or less the same beliefs. On the other hand, she was extremely well up on anything of a superstitious nature that was given a green light by the priests. For example, if you received Holy Communion on nine consecutive first Fridays of the month, you were assured that you would not die without the ministrations of a priest. Other benefits would come your way if you were to walk seven times around a particular church while reciting prescribed prayers. There was a whole list of similar superstitious rites that, when carried out in the proper fashion and the correct number of times, guaranteed certain results. One of the real causes of confusion for me was when she would issue one of her favourite dictums: that because so-and-so 'only goes to Mass when it suits him', he would 'never have luck'.

She was in fact a class of a pagan, but I suppose there isn't anything wrong with that either.

During the time I lived with my granny, from the age of about three until I was twenty-one, I was to hear vague but persistent rumblings from my aunts, and also my mother, that Nanny had things wrong with her. She suffered from her 'nerves'. Kidney trouble was also mentioned. In general she was considered to be 'delicate'. She lived until she was ninety-three.

Whenever Nanny announced that one of her ailments was at her, my aunts and even my grandfather would prescribe 'a drop of whiskey'. *Sure, it'll do you good.* She would then, with downcast eyes, and fiddling with her wedding ring, say something like, 'Ah sure, I think I'm not long for this world, but if yez all think that it would do me good I might as well try a drop. But only a drop, mind.'

I would then be sent to Mr Taggart, a grocer who also had an off-licence, to get a naggin of Power's Whiskey, and 'Don't be there till you're back.'

When she had taken some of her medicine she certainly had the appearance of having miraculously recovered from whatever had ailed her. She would become talkative and even funny, recounting stories of the time she had been a maid in one of the big houses on the seafront – 'The master had said this, the master had said that'; talking about the time her father had seen the ghost and how he had 'never overed it'; recalling memories of her life as a young woman and telling us stories of characters and customs that had disappeared. She would sing half-remembered songs and reminisce about her own family, most of whom had long since died.

These little soirées were not all that frequent, because, remember, she was a very delicate woman and had 'turns' quite often. I really enjoyed these interludes and still look back on them with a very warm feeling.

St Malachy was an old Irish saint, much given to foretelling things. He was a kind of Irish Nostradamus. I'm sure that somewhere in his predictions he foretold happy events, but I have never heard of any of them. This is not very surprising because my only knowledge of

St Malachy was gleaned from my granny, who, when in melancholic mood, which was fairly often, would quote at great length from 'the prophesies', telling us the signs and omens that were to serve as a warning to all that the end of the world was fast approaching. Phrases laden with doom – 'Man will not know the difference in the seasons, except for the leaves on the trees' or 'People will be driven mad by the roar of the sea' and many other dictums of the same ilk – would be delivered with all the expertise of an actress well versed in melo-drama. Instinctively I knew that she enjoyed these performances. What I couldn't figure out was why: how could anyone actually enjoy imparting such terrible news?

Her melancholic phrases were perhaps understandable when it is taken into consideration that her first-born was a girl called Kitty who had died, before I was born, from what I think must have been consumption. She was twenty-one when she died and was considered by the whole family as having been the most beautiful girl in Ireland. In all probability this was not the case, but then we all have ways of dealing with our grief. It was often said by the six remaining children and her husband that she had never got over Kitty's death.

I have no doubt that Nanny's grief was real. I also believe that had she re-engaged in what had been her normal life up until the death of her daughter, her grief would have been assuaged, at least to a manageable level, and she could have lived a reasonably contented life, which would of course have included periods of sadness of the sort which we all for one reason or another have to put up with.

However, in their efforts to protect her and to shield her from any day-to-day worries or unpleasantness of any sort, and though their motives were admirable, the entire family saw to it that she was never to enjoy such a normal life again. Her daughters took over the running of the house and she was not allowed to lift a hand in the area of cleaning, cooking, polishing, etc. And this, whether we like it or not, was what constituted the normal life of a working-class woman in those days. They meant well. Or maybe they felt guilty because the death of their sister had not hit them as hard as it had hit their mother, and they felt it to be their duty to employ their energies in trying to alleviate the relentless grief which they felt their mother was suffering. Whatever the reasons – and I am making no attempt to lay blame on one side or the other – that's just the way it was. And if there's a heaven I hope they are all in it.

The years I spent living in that house were not all doom and gloom, though I must admit that there was a fair bit of it about, not only in the house but in Ireland generally. The period I spent there included the late thirties, the forties and most of the fifties, a period in Irish history not noted for its joyfulness or gay abandon. Having said all that there were very enjoyable times as well, like when Uncle Paddy came home from sea with presents and stories, and the nights when Nanny would have 'a drop' of whiskey as a cure for whatever ailed her. And Christmas was hugely enjoyable because around that time I would meet all my cousins and other relations. Also at Christmas my own father and mother and brothers and sisters would spend the evening there. They lived only about two miles away, so I saw quite a lot of them, but not as much as I would have liked. Uncle Eddie would play the piano and various aunts and uncles would sing Irish songs and music hall songs.

Then there were the funerals to which I was taken. This was a big source of entertainment. First you had to read the death notices to know if there was a funeral you needed to go to. The *Irish Independent* was the paper my grandfather would buy on his way home from Mass. In those days, you could almost tell which political party a family supported by the paper they read. The working class, even the upwardly moving working class, would have considered buying the *Irish Times* as 'getting above' yourself. That left two other daily newspapers. The *Independent* was seen to be the paper of Fine Gael, not for its biased political views but because it was believed by the upwardly moving crowd that the people involved in the Fine Gael party were a more refined type, certainly not so rampantly republican as that De Valera crowd, which was too bloody Irish altogether. That left the *Irish Press*, Fianna Fáil's paper, and there was no doubt about the political affiliation of the people who read *that* paper.

In each of these newspapers was column after column of death notices. My grandfather would read 'the Deaths' with great attention, reading aloud the names and funeral arrangements of any Dún Laoghaire person who featured. From time to time Nanny would announce,

'I'll have to go to that funeral; didn't I know her well, Lord have mercy on her.'

I would be sent at once to Mr Keegan. Mr Keegan was a cabman who lived in a lane at the top of Marine Road, facing St Michael's Church. Opposite his house were large stables in which he kept a few horses and his cabs. I would be sent by my granny to inform Mr Keegan that she needed a cab for the next morning and he was to make sure that he would be in good time to take her to ten o'clock Mass and later to the funeral at Dean's Grange Cemetery.

For some reason I never really understood, I was kept home from school to accompany her to these funerals. Mr Keegan would arrive in his cab and herself would be ready to step into it. Insofar as I could see, she only ever dressed in black clothes and of course a black hat, so she was always ready for the off, as it were, when it came to funerals. When my granny and myself got into the cab, there was always another old lady already ensconced. I wouldn't have known or cared very much who she was, but on one particular day I somehow found out that she was Mr Keegan's wife.

On that day, when the person had been buried and all the prayers said, the three of us took our places in the cab again. The cabman had taken a right turn at the cemetery gates and we were heading for home. I was glad because, while I enjoyed a jaunt in the cab, I was getting a bit tired of the sound of two old women chattering away. Their voices sometimes dropped to a whisper, which caused me to turn towards them. When this happened I was told, gently but firmly, to 'keep lookin' out the window, you, and don't be tryin' to listen to women's talk'. About five hundred yards on we were coming to a crossroads where a left turn would take us to Dún Laoghaire, but before we could turn left my grandmother pulled me by the sleeve and handed me a ten shilling note. 'Shout up to Mr Keegan and tell him to give the horse a rest here and give him that money and tell him to get a pint for himself and then you get out of the cab and amuse yourself.'

I was amusing myself by kicking stones or messing about in some way when I noticed Mr Keegan coming out of the pub carrying two small glasses which I knew to be whiskey; he handed these to the two women through the open window of the cab. A short time later I saw him leaving the pub to collect the two glasses from the ladies and return them inside. Then he resumed his position in the driving seat and we were heading for home. Or so I thought.

The homeward journey from this pub started by the horse having to pull the cab and us up a steepish hill. At the time I didn't think it was a very steep hill – for a horse – but my granny and her companion were of the opinion that the hill was very steep indeed. 'That poor horse must be wore out from pullin' us up the hill. It wouldn't be Christian not to tell him to give the animal a rest.' We had arrived at another crossroads, which happened to have a pub on one of its corners. So the performance from the first pub got a re-run, only this time Mr Keegan made two trips from the pub to the cab with the 'drops of the craythur'. I think we had two more stops before we arrived home, and as we were leaving the cab the two ladies took leave of one another with great formality: 'Goodbye, Mrs Keegan, and mind yourself.' 'Goodbye, Mrs Maher, and you mind yourself too.' (My lasting memory of the cabman, Mr Keegan, is that on that day I did not hear him speak one word. I wondered if maybe he was dumb but at a later time in another place I heard him talking to my grandfather, so it turned out he could speak after all.)

When my granny and I came into the house, I was hoping that my aunts would prescribe a 'drop of something' to help revive her after her arduous day at the funeral; and so it turned out, and the result was that we had a very pleasant few hours. In all fairness, she could handle it; there was no staggering or slurring of words. The only sign that she had had a drop was a bright little spot of red on each cheek.

Chapter 4

I started my working life as a trainee electrician. My father was a carpenter, and working on building sites he knew a lot of the contractors. He knew this contractor, Mr Hill, who had an electrical business and he got me a job with him as an apprentice. After about nine months, Mr Hill rang my father and said, 'Paddy, this boy doesn't seem to be interested in this work.' So my father said, 'Well, sack him.' So I was sacked. I learnt a few things but nothing of any great value.

Then I was apprenticed to a man called Wally Knowles in this factory in Sallynoggin. There was a man from Yorkshire used to run it and he wasn't very friendly – put it that way – so that didn't last.

There was great hope for me when I got a position as a draper's assistant. They hoped I'd train in that job and become an official draper. It was half in the blood. My aunt Eileen Maher was a cutter of clothes for women. And she used to make stuff at home for some women, but only very special women. And she'd charge them next to nothing. Apparently she was a very fine cutter, which is very important in the making of clothes, I'm told.

I like a good suit myself. You see when I was young, I was always wanting a suit but I never got one, a real one, that I liked. And Crombie overcoats were all the thing in those days and I was looking for one of them. One day they announced they were bringing me into town to get me a Crombie. I got this coat that was cut the same way as a Crombie but it wasn't a Crombie. I knew the minute I looked at it. It was a pretend one. So when I did get to get a suit I said I'd get a good suit.

Anyway, the story with my career in the drapery business is that I ended up closing the shop. It was up beside the vegetable market in North King Street. It was called the Spinning Wheel and it was horrendous: the place was falling asunder and I used to have to go down the stairs and sweep out the cellar. But first I had to put my trousers down my socks because of the rats down there. Farmers would come in to be measured for a suit, but I don't think they must have been too particular about the fit. As long as it was kind of near it would be all right. I was really the 'gofer' of the place: when the messenger boy wasn't there I'd be sent out on the messenger boy's bike with stuff. Because I was only a small fry, I wasn't allowed to have my lunch on the premises, so I used to eat around in Halston Street Church and then I'd go for a walk. And one day I ended up walking past the Gate Theatre and opposite was a Georgian house and in the fanlight was 'Union of Distributive Workers and Clerks'. So I went in and I told them how much I was getting and the union official was horror stricken. I had to pay six shillings for a ticket to go from Dún Laoghaire into Nelson's Pillar. And so that left fourteen shillings and I more of less had to give up that at home. I only got about two or three shillings for myself. I was getting a bit fed up with it. He said I should have been getting something like £2 a week. He said to me, find out what all the other people are getting, and come back and tell us. So I did.

One day the manager came out when he got the bill from the union. He said, 'Who's responsible for this?'

I said, 'I am.'

'Well,' he said, 'I'm never speaking to you again.' I think I was supposed to be mortally hurt. I got the money that the union demanded they give me. It was like forty quid or something. And the others got back-pay as well, some of them going back years. In hindsight I don't blame the manager of the place because he probably had a family and he was afraid of his life the place would shut down. The people who owned the place were from Ennis; they used to come up every week, collect money and skedaddle out of the place. It closed down shortly after.

I went to work in Brooks Thomas in the electrical department. The whole ceiling was covered with all these different light fittings and things. One day this man came in from the country and he pointed to one, and then another, and said I'd like one of them and one of them and one of them and so on. He said it's for a new house and it's not even built yet. I thought he'd come back to order, that there was bound to be a discussion. But he just came in one day and said, have you got my stuff? I said no and he kicked up murder. The manager of our department called me in and said the customer is always right. Well, I said, in this case he was wrong. I was sent up to face three directors – you'd think I was a bigwig in the place, not just a young fellow working on the shop floor. They said, 'Drew, if this continues we'll have to let you go.'

Well, I said, if you want to let me go you might as well let me go today – it's a nice fine day – provided you give me the two weeks' holiday money in lieu. They couldn't understand my cheek, because from their point of view I should have been in terror. But I wasn't. I never thought about the future, never thought, how am I going to get a job to retirement out of this.

The 1950s in Ireland was a very bad period for those of the population dependent on work as a means of keeping body and soul together. There was not a lot of it to be had. As a consequence, queues were forming all over the country outside of the Labour Exchange offices, so that the workless could get inside to 'sign on'.

The daily signing on procedure was meant to be proof, at least to the bureaucrats, that you did not have a job and that you were therefore truly unemployed and available for employment, in which case they – the agents of the social welfare system – could, with a clear conscience, and without fear of reprimand from a supervisor, make payment to you of your financial entitlement each Friday.

In 1955 I joined the Dún Laoghaire queue, which meant that for the first time I was 'on the labour'. Even though it was well known to the population as a whole that work was very scarce, nevertheless there was a kind of stigma attached to being the recipient of unemployment benefit, and there were – particularly among the better off, and even among some of the working-class citizens, who were themselves in secure employment – vague rumblings of a holier than thou nature. 'Work-shy.' 'Oh, on the labour, I believe.' 'Of course, was never known to be too fond of work, even during the good times.' 'Very fond of drink.' 'Never goes near church, chapel or meeting.' Etc. Signing on was a big black mark against you.

23

The time spent by me on the labour was mercifully short, about three months, but I did have what turned out to be an interesting few weeks, during which I made the acquaintance of a man who turned out to be a great teller of tales, and I gleaned from his conversation that he may actually have been one of the genuinely work-shy.

He had worked in England, he told me, but sure working 'over there' on the building of roads, and on building sites, would have been enough to kill a horse, never mind a man. 'I mean to say, I have no objection to working for a living, but I'll be damned if I'm going to work with nothin' but death staring me in the face.' He also said that he felt very lonely over there, and that to while away the long dark evenings he took to reading a lot. 'I even got as far as reading big thick books, in fact one day a fella gave me a book to read. It was written, I was told, by an Irishman. Well, all I can say is, he must have been a very quare Paddy, because I could hardly make head nor tail of it, and the bits that I could understand were so filthy and disgraceful that they couldn't possibly have happened in Ireland. Sure, isn't it a well-known fact that this is a good Catholic country and we have the respect of the world, everywhere? Now, I'm not sayin' we're saints but at the same time you must admit that we know where to draw the line.' The book, it turned out, was *Ulysses*.

Another fellow I met at this time was an individual so fed up with not being able to find gainful employment that he told me he was going to join the French Foreign Legion. I discovered later that he did join up and that after a few years he was invalided out, came back to Ireland and lived on the pension he received from the Legion.

I tried for a few weeks to get work of any description, an effort which was severely thwarted by the fact that I didn't have any particular skills and I never had any ambition to do anything. I didn't have any leaning or any direction. All they spoke about in the national school was getting scholarships and working in Guinness', as far as I could see. Working in Guinness' was a good job at the time, I suppose, if you want to. But I just couldn't look forward at all. And I didn't have any ambition. I don't know why. I was just a very dreamy sort of character.

At that time, I had an uncle who had worked for many years as a clerk in the General Post Office in Dublin, and he suggested to me that I might make an application for a job as a male night telephonist, because he had heard on the grapevine that there could possibly be a vacancy in this capacity at the Central Telephone Exchange. It would not of course be an ideal job, he pointed out, because as the daytime operations of the exchange were carried out entirely by women, men were required to work only by night, which meant I would – that is 'if I were lucky enough to get a position' – be working very unsociable hours, but, as I didn't have much of a social life in any case, 'sure wouldn't anything be better than being on the labour'. So I applied for this position by writing a letter that contained a sizeable dollop of fiction regarding my previous experience in the workforce.

When I had not received any reply after a few weeks of waiting, I became disheartened and decided that there was only one solution to the problem, and that was to take what I, along with thousands of others, felt was the only option available: to take the boat for England.

There were at that time three Mail Packet Steamers, or, in layman's language, 'mail-boats', plying between Dún Laoghaire and Holyhead in Wales – the *Hibernia*, the *Cambria* and the *Princess Maud*. You did not of course have any choice in the matter of which boat you sailed on – you just had to travel on whichever boat was making the crossing on the particular night that you had decided to leave – but the one most people dreaded was the *Maud*, because stories had reached us via veteran travellers that no matter how calm conditions seemed there would always be a swell when you got outside of the harbour, and that however slight the swell appeared the *Maud* would not be able to handle it and that she would be 'buckin' and leppin'' for the whole trip.

The embarkation point was the Carlisle Pier in Dún Laoghaire Harbour. This was a functional piece of Victorian construction, its entire length covered by a canopy-like pitched roof supported by ornate iron columns. Every evening a train enveloped in steam would slowly come to a halt under this roof with a cargo of passengers who had earlier travelled to Dublin from all parts of the country to catch this train and be taking the boat.

It was easier and less expensive for me, because, being a resident of Dún Laoghaire, I simply had to walk to the pier and buy a ticket, which enabled me to travel by the mail-boat and to take the connecting train to London's Euston Station for the sum of £3.

This was my first time to have left home. I was seen off by some of my family, and even though I was twenty-one years old, I was a very young twenty-one. With the benefit of hindsight I now realize that I was terribly immature and inexperienced and probably the equivalent of a young teenager nowadays.

Carrying my small case along the poorly lighted pier on a damp, smelly, chilly and dreary evening, I had a great sense of desolation and loneliness. Not knowing what lay ahead, I was also feeling frightened. And then I became deeply ashamed because emerging from the steam-shrouded train, making their way towards the gangway alongside me, were young fellows of no more than sixteen or seventeen. They seemed generally to be in good spirits and to my way of thinking they were handling their impending exile like real men, and here was I, a twenty-one-year-old on the point of tears. I was suddenly in dread that they would be able to read from my face what was going on in my head. I hadn't heard of the word 'machismo' at that time.

A great many of the people who had to leave in the fifties would have had some member of their family, an uncle, a cousin or a brother, already living and working in England, probably for one of the big construction or civil engineering companies. Some would have been tradesmen – carpenters, bricklayers and so on – but the vast majority would have been, as they were called in that pre-politically correct age, builders' labourers. Although England was being more or less refurbished after the war and there was plenty of work to be had on the numerous construction sites, it was an advantage to have a relative there, as he could probably get you a job at the site where he was working himself, help you to find accommodation and generally show you the ropes. In this way you were spared having to waste time and money on these preliminaries.

Even though I had come from a long line of tradesmen, mainly carpenters, who had long experience of the building trade, and would have been very well-up in which tactic to use when seeking work on a building site, they did not see fit to give me any advice before I set off. Now, this was not due to any lack of interest in my well-being, far from it, because for years they had been dispensing advice as to what courses of action I needed to take if I wanted to remain a part of the human race, and to go about earning my living in a decent normal way, which had been the lot of many a good man before me and would be after me. I think it was like the case that their advice-giving had reached saturation point, and that they had probably tacitly agreed amongst themselves that I was a contrary oddity: '*Sure, he goes about the place dreamin', readin' funny books and askin' questions that the pope couldn't or wouldn't bother answerin'. He's as odd as two left boots and contrary with it, and no matter what you say to him he'll just go his own way, so we might as well just let him off and hope to God no real harm comes to him.*' In other words, they were resigned to the fact that what they were dealing with was a very odd little bollix indeed.

Advice or no advice, I continued to the edge of the pier, walked up the gangway and onto the deck of the ship. Almost as soon as my feet touched the deck the cloud of doom and gloom which surrounded me was pierced by a thin sliver of light; it was what I now realize was a sense of adventure.

As I walked along the deck of the ship details of my new environment added to my sense of adventure. There were sailors dressed in what was then the traditional garb of the mariner: peakless white caps with a blue headband, on the front of which was emblazoned the name of the ship, S.S. *Hibernia*, in gold lettering. Hanging from the back of the cap was a blue ribbon and they also wore navy-blue bell-bottomed trousers. There was a deck all caulked and dowelled, the lifeboats, the white-painted superstructure, the narrow companionways, and the wheelings and reelings of the gulls.

When I had taken in all this, my next port of call was to be the bar, which, in spite of the unfamiliarity of my surroundings, I managed to find with surprising ease. As soon as I went into the bar, I began to feel at home, because it appeared to be much the same as many a pub in which I had had a drink on land. There was a bar with stools along its length, fixed benches around the walls, and out on the floor there were a few tables and chairs. It was all very functional and there was no attempt to create any kind of atmosphere. I suppose they reckoned that the patrons would create their own atmosphere when they had enough drink in them, which was exactly what happened, at least the night I happened to be there.

As most of the customers in the bar had, prior to embarkation, partaken of several parting glasses to dull the pain of their imminent departure from Paddy's Green Shamrock Shore, it was only about twenty minutes into the voyage that the inevitable melodeon made its appearance. Very soon after came a couple of fiddles and flutes (guitars had not yet become an acceptable instrument within Irish Music circles). The reels and jigs were belted out with great enthusiasm and whether or not they were technically good musicians I don't remember, but they played with verve and feeling and they helped to assuage the loneliness that most of us had been feeling a short time before.

Now, while most of us had never met one another before, during the trip an easy familiarity grew up between us, helped, no doubt, by the drink. Shortly after the high-spirited music and our own high-spirited enjoyment of it, there was an abrupt mood swing. There seemed to be a general unspoken agreement that as we had all left Ireland and were halfway across the Irish Sea we were exiles already and as such were entitled to feel homesick. This expressed itself in the playing of plaintive laments and the singing of various dirges and blatantly sentimental songs. This continued until we arrived at Holyhead.

On arrival, myself and the rest of the merrymakers from the bar headed for the outside deck, walked down the gangway and were once again on terra firma. Even though it was a different terra firma to the one we had so recently left, the surroundings and the atmosphere were remarkably similar. As we made our shambling progress along the quay to the platform from which trains departed for different destinations all over England, the conviviality and camaraderie which had come into being on the boat dwindled at about the same pace as the effects of the drink.

At the convergence of the quay and the railway platform, there was a dimly lit café. It was around about midnight and, as the train on which I was to travel to London was not due to leave for nearly an hour, I went into the café and partook of what I was later to hear disparagingly referred to as British Railways tea. While I sat there, making a concerted effort to dispel the negative effects of the black cloud which had once again settled over me, suddenly my thoughts were broken into by an announcement over the public address system, to the effect that 'The train now standing at Platform 3 will depart for London Euston at 12.51 a.m.'

As I meandered towards Platform 3, I began to wonder why it was that railway trains ran to such a very strict timetable. What I mean to say is that during the normal course of our social behaviour we make appointments for say 12.30 or 12.45 and if we happen to turn up a few minutes later than the appointed time, it's not generally regarded as an act of such irresponsibility as to warrant a severe finger wagging. Then I came to the realization that the whole railway timetable thing was a confidence trick. It was designed to convey to the ordinary Joe Soap that, while he might be casual or lackadaisical in his approach to travel, or indeed other areas of his life, he was now dealing with a company whose logistical genius and efficiency was an undisputable fact and not to be questioned.

The train left at 12.58. After a long and tedious journey, marked only by its misery and by my attempts at fitful sleep, I emerged from Euston Station onto the streets of London. It was about 6.30 a.m. and, as I stood outside the station, I looked around in a kind of numbed state and I experienced a new sensation – shock.

It was a very run-down area and most of the buildings seemed to be cheap lodging houses, dingy offices and not-very-inviting-looking cafés, most of which were not yet open. There was a very grimy and sordid feel to the whole place. In my immediate vicinity I noticed pitiful mounds of makeshift bedding, under which lay those members of our supposedly Christian society who had lost any aspirations or hope that they might at one time have had, and who had now given up the fight.

This sight did not, I am ashamed to say, awaken any feelings of compassion in me for these people. All I felt was the selfish hope that I would not end up like these poor unfortunates, living on the streets.

Chapter 5

In London it never occurred to me to go to the buildings: I probably didn't want to do the work. I said to other lads what would you do about getting a job and they said there's a place that sells vacuum cleaners and they give you a week's training first. I went to that and I did the week's training and I laughed my way through that because I figured the guy giving the training thought everybody was a fool in the world. It was all about sales patter and all that stuff. I didn't do any good at that. I went out for a week and never sold a single vacuum cleaner and that was the end of me. After that I got jobs in hotels. I was a kitchen porter in two hotels. I was a lift man in another.

I didn't have any real fixed abode. There were a few fellows I knew over there and I'd stay with some of them, different places from week to week to week. If I stayed for a week or two, I'd pay my contribution towards the rent. It was mainly sleeping on the floor. We didn't have any money to go out drinking or anything like that. Every now and again we'd get a few pints, but all in all we hadn't got much money. I was playing a little bit of music and going to gigs. There was a famous folk club called the Troubadour on the Brompton Road and I went along, but they had no room for another fellow, so that was that. I just worked.

One evening I arrived home from my job in the Mount Royal Hotel in Marble Arch to find a letter waiting for me. It had come from one of my aunts informing me that there had been a communication from the Department of Posts and Telegraphs and that I was to present myself at the G.P.O. on Monday morning for an interview, and that everybody knew that when you were called for an interview in any government department 'the job was as good as got'.

After just a few months, this was to be my last day as Paddy in London.

I was a lift man in the Mount Royal. I was dressed in a grey suit with brass buttons and a black trim, and my task was to ask the guests which floor they wanted and to take them there by operating a kind of lever on the wall of the lift; not a very challenging job, you might say, and so would I. This day happened to be Friday, so that when my shift ended, which was at four o'clock in the afternoon, I collected my wages of £7 and set off to walk up Bayswater Road to Sussex Gardens, where I was then sharing a flat with three other fellows. It was not a flat in the strict sense of the word, but that's what we called it for the sake of decency; it was a room, a very big room, on the second floor of a large three-storey Victorian or Edwardian house (I'm never sure about this period thing).

The room had been rented in the name of one of the lads, who in turn sublet, as it were, spaces to the other three at a very reasonable rate. The place was furnished, which meant it had one bed, a couple of sofas, a few chairs and a table. There was a fair supply of blankets with which we covered ourselves upon retiring, whether on one of the sofas or on the floor; the sleeping arrangements were on a first-come, first-served basis. The bed could only be slept in by the guy in whose name the flat was rented; this unspoken rule was observed not out of consideration or respect but because he was a hell of a lot bigger than the rest of us. In the fireplace was a single gas ring, which was used solely for boiling the kettle to make tea. On the landing outside the room we had a bathroom in which very few baths were taken, because, although it had a water-heating device called a geyser, it was an awful long wait until the water was sufficiently hot for the purpose of taking a bath. In general the bathroom was used for washing underpants and socks, which you hoped would be dry enough when a change of these items became necessary. My outside clothes consisted of what I stood up in, but mercifully they didn't show the dirt. It wasn't an ideal place to live, but then not much living was done there. It was first and foremost a place to throw the head down and nobody ever sat around relaxing in the place. As we were all young we didn't really notice the near squalid conditions in which we were living.

Before I had finished reading the letter from home, I knew that on Saturday evening I would head for Euston Station to catch the boat-train for Holyhead and thence to Dún Laoghaire, where any kind of responsibility would be a thing of the past. I was delighted, not as you might think because I was going home to a good job, but because I had an excuse to leave England and to return to Ireland where, selfish little bollix that I was, I would be returning to a life of comparative ease. Meals would be handed to me, clothes would be washed, and I would have a nice bed to sleep in, and even if the job in the Telephone Exchange didn't work out no one would accuse me of shirking.

I gave no thought to the hopes and aspirations that the entire family – my mother, my father, grandfather, grandmother and my aunts – had for me or to my future, which, if it was now secured in the form of a good job, would have brought them a great feeling of achievement and would be a vindication of the undoubted sacrifices they had made on my behalf through many years.

I gave no thought to the hotel where I had worked for a few weeks and where I had been treated very kindly. It never occurred to me that I should, before leaving their employ, have given them a week's notice that I was leaving, to which they were entitled, nor, having received the intelligence about the job in the Telephone Exchange, that there and then I should have gone to see them – even to tell them some lie about having been called home because of a family crisis and that I had no option but to leave immediately, and to thank them for their kindness. Such consideration would have occurred to any normal, less self-absorbed person.

I wouldn't even miss the lads with whom, for several weeks, I had shared a living space. It would be true to say that the four of us had not become close to one another or come close to establishing any real camaraderie. But nevertheless we had lived together after a fashion for a few weeks and we had, on occasion, had a few pints together; it should have meant something. It's hard to believe but I don't even remember their names.

Thanks be to God I did not have to wait too long to diagnose this ugly selfishness in myself and so was able to begin to deal with it: I'm probably still dealing with it, but at least now I recognize it and if I feel or see it approaching I can start to stamp it out. Was it any wonder I didn't, as a young fellow, have a circle of friends?

*

Arriving at Holyhead, the place that on my journey to London a couple of months earlier had seemed a most depressing place, now felt quite pleasant; but then I was on my way home this time. I arrived at Dún Laoghaire very early on Sunday morning with only a couple of pounds in my pocket. I had had a few pints in the bar and felt in good form; the drink at that time was enjoyable and had not taken the hold it was to take in later years. I made straight for the granny's house, where I was welcomed with the kind of gusto which I thought was reserved for people who had been away for years, not a couple of months; nevertheless, I lapped it up.

After a very lavish breakfast the letter from the Department of Posts and Telegraphs was produced and discussed. My interview at the G.P.O. was scheduled for 11 a.m. on Monday morning. I pointed out that the post for which I was being interviewed was that of a T.M.N.T., which meant a 'temporary male night telephonist', and that the word 'temporary' implied that the job might only last a few weeks. This idea was pooh-poohed with stuff like, 'Once you get a foot in the door of any government job and don't dirty your bib, you'll be there forever; sure look at Uncle Eddie, didn't he start in the Post Office as a temporary and now he's a kind of a boss in there, and a damn good pension to look forward to. No, you go into that interview tomorrow, put your best foot forward, make a good impression and mark my words, you'll have a job for life.'

Next morning I reached the G.P.O. in good time armed with my Primary Cert., the reference from the Christian Brothers where I went to secondary school up to but not including the Intermediate Certificate, and one from the Dún Laoghaire technical school which I attended after the Christian Brothers. I had read these references and I suppose the teachers who had written them had tried to be kind, but reading between the lines even I felt them to be very dubious. There was heavy emphasis on how honest I was and how I did my best, but I imagine they contained a kind of coded message to prospective employers that they would be ill advised to employ me at anything that presented any kind of intellectual challenge.

After a short wait I was shown into an office where I waited for an interview with a Posts and Telegraphs manager. At the close of the interview he told me I had secured the position as a T.M.N.T., but that I would first of all have to attend a two weeks' training course, the details of which would be sent on to me by post, and in the meantime I was to present myself in the G.P.O. on the following Thursday for a medical. Now the idea of having to have a medical examination struck the fear of God into me. As a child I did not like vegetables of any kind and in their efforts to get me to eat them the ladies in my life – my mother, my aunts and my grandmother – regularly issued dire warnings: 'If you don't eat up your cabbage we'll bring you to the doctor and he'll stick needles in you and send you to hospital where you'll have to eat plates of cabbage every day.' I'm sure that what they were trying to impress on me was that eating vegetables would be good for my general health, but somehow they sent out a very mixed message. Instead of frightening me into eating cabbage and other vegetables, it caused me to be terrified of doctors and hospitals. The result was that when I presented myself at the G.P.O. for my medical I was in terror. But I needn't have worried because it took only about three minutes; it was a 'listen-to-the-heart, look-into-the-ears-and-eyes, stick-your-tongue-out-and-say-"Aaaahhhh", and you're in' kind of a medical.

Everybody was very excited when I got a job in the Telephone Exchange. This was far better than they'd ever hoped for. A job with security, eventually a pension, and you wouldn't have to wear overalls going to work; you'd be the next best thing to a gentleman.

The next step on my journey was the cramming course, which consisted of tuition in the use of the headset. There is a version of this piece of equipment still extant – and it may be seen on the heads of pretty young ladies in offices and hotels – and it consists of an earpiece and a mouthpiece at the end of a slim wire and is an extremely dainty item. However, the headset of which I speak was in two parts: the part worn on the head, which incorporated two earpieces, was like a horse collar and then there was a speaking tube, like some other piece of horse paraphernalia, that hung from a strap worn around the neck and rested on the chest.

The trainers placed great emphasis on the bureaucratic procedures involved in the job: there was a special way to pass numbers to another exchange; people who dialled the exchange were 'subscribers'; in the event of you being insubordinate in any way you would be issued with an M.P.1.8. notification, which contained a charge that had to be answered in writing . . . and so on – the list seemed to go on forever. Mercifully this training course lasted only two weeks, after which we became fully fledged telephonists and were let loose on the citizens who wished to communicate with each other.

Chapter 6

From the minute I became a fully fledged telephone operator my world changed dramatically for the better: for the first time in my life I felt I fitted in. Up to now I had been a solitary individual, at least in my interests. While my contemporaries were listening to and discussing what was then called the hit parade, I was listening to *Ceolta Tíre*, a programme of Irish music presented by Ciarán MacMathúna. Another of my favourite programmes was called *Ballad Makers' Saturday Night*. From listening to these programmes I developed a great interest in Ireland's music, its songs and its history. By the time I was in my early twenties I had learned a good few songs and I had also been learning how to play guitar, an instrument on which I was never to become a virtuoso.

My father would have been sort of a jazzer. He would have loved all the Bing Crosby and all those fellows – Big Band and all that. And my mother would have been similar. So my interest in Irish music all came about afterwards – just playing the guitar and being able to accompany myself a bit got me going on it. As the time went on I got more and more interested in Irish music. I began to get very interested in the songs and particularly where they came from, and I also got very interested in the themes of songs. There were love songs and war songs and then fellows-being-deported-for-having-robbed-a-rabbit songs.

I took up the guitar after going to a film with a friend of mine called Pat McMahon. It was the first time I heard authentic flamenco. In Hollywood films there was plenty of castanets and plenty of show, but not the real stuff. When I heard the real thing I thought it was great music. So I took up the guitar and I went to this body and that

4

this resulted in my being was a solitary individual at least in my interests, While my contemporaries were listening to and discussing what was then called the "Hit Parade" I was listening to Ceolta Tíre a programme of Irish music presented by Ciarán Mac Mathúna and also another of my favourite programmes was called "Ballad makers Saturday night" from listening to these programmes I developed a great interest in Irelands music its songs and its history.

By the time I was in my early twenties I had learned a good few songs, and I had also been learning how to play guitar an instrument on which I was never to become a virtuoso, my Real body for lessons but it was afterwards when I got to Spain and went for lessons that I really got interested in it.

I had read quite a lot between the ages of sixteen and nineteen, but the books I had read had been mainly of a religious content. Catholicism was such a dominant factor in the Ireland of the fifties it became for me a puzzle. I never met anyone else at that time who had any questions to ask; no doubt there were some about but I never met them. My questioning was regarded as heretical and indeed blasphemous. For example I would ask the simplest of questions: how could boys and girls – who, we were told by the Church, reached the age of reason at seven – be allowed to make their First Holy Communion, during which they would recite the Hail Mary, while not knowing what a womb was? Or indeed what conception was? And I could never understand Catholic people saying, for instance, say so many Hail Marys and you'll have great luck. Luck and religion don't go together. I was very confused in areas like that. It seemed to have been generally accepted by the Catholic population that, while they acknowledged the Seven Deadly Sins, and the Ten Commandments, there were really only two sins – taking advantage of a young wan up a lane and the other was thinking about it.

When I was very young I had thought about becoming a priest, but I couldn't reconcile the way the priests were living and the way the poor were living. I ended up having a lot of respect for the Cistercian order. Because they didn't speak and they stayed inside their monastery and they carried out the rule of St Benedict and so on. To this day I like them. They don't just do things by rote, they're all men who think. And by think I don't mean ponderously all the time thinking for the sake of it but they do try to figure things out.

The reason that working in the Telephone Exchange changed my life so radically was that there were a lot of people there who – in the restrictive society in which I had lived up until the time I went to England – would have been described as 'odd balls'. These were people who questioned authority – the Church, the establishment and the general status quo at the time. In other words, they would have been looked upon as anarchists and communists, even though the people throwing around these labels would never have understood what constituted an anarchist, and as for communism, the Church condemned it so that was the end of it.

So at the Telephone Exchange I got to know fellows who had interesting ideas and read books and that sort of thing. I wouldn't go so far as to say I was on some sort of intellectual quest, but I was full of questions – questions that up until then I had asked but people thought they were stupid questions. And then I met these people and they regarded the questions as valid questions.

For my part I was delighted to have fallen in with these so-called eccentrics, because when I would tentatively express an idea or ask a question or put forward a theory I would not be answered by a snigger. The Telephone Exchange is where it all started, where I had an opportunity to voice my opinion and have it taken a bit seriously by other people. The man who influenced me most was probably Michael Kane, a fine painter and extremely well read and an intellectual. He was the very first man to listen seriously to what I had to say.

I had made a lot of friends in the exchange, aspiring painters, poets, actors, writers and so on. Joe Hackett was a poet and I met him through Michael Kane. Joe was in the Exchange but he had been to Spain. And there was John Kelly, another painter. John wasn't in the Exchange but he'd also been in Spain. The area most frequented by us all was Leeson Street, Baggot Street, down to Grafton Street and all the streets off it, with the occasional excursion to the Gate Theatre and the pubs around Parnell Street.

I'd stayed in the Telephone Exchange for close on a year when I realized that this pension everyone was so keen on would not be collected for about forty years, and this great security business they were on about was becoming a bit of a pain in the arse, so I decided to part company with the Telephone Exchange. This was not a decision I arrived at all on my own. You see, one night, I was sitting with my headset on. I was what was called 'taking calls'. In those days people had to dial 'o' to get onto the Exchange and then they would hear 'Number please?' and they would say the number of the phone they wanted to get through to and would be put through. In front of me was a kind of wall and on it were rows and rows of small red and white lights. When somebody called, a light came on and underneath each light was a small hole and when you put a plug into one of these holes, the light went out and the caller was connected. On occasion there were delays, which meant that it might take a long time to get through.

One evening a lady came on looking for a call to London. I knew by the sound of her that she was a bombastic oul' bitch. So I was delighted to be able to tell her that she would have to join a kind of virtual queue, as the lines to London were overloaded and that there would be a delay of one and a half hours. At this, she blew her top and started to rant and rave. *Disgraceful! Ridiculous! And I'll see about this! This is a very urgent call!* I explained that urgent in Telephone Exchange parlance had a very different meaning than urgent in the ordinary sense of the word. It meant that only a government minister could jump the queue, and would she ever go and fuck off and not be annoying me.

This, as you can imagine, really stoked up her engine. *How dare you! Disgraceful . . . rudeness . . . put in your place . . . sacked!*

She then said, 'Young man, do you realize to whom you are speaking?'

'No, madam.'

'I am the wife of the Minister for Posts and Telegraphs and I will complain most severely about your attitude and your behaviour. It is disgraceful!'

I then said, 'Do you realize, madam, to whom you are speaking?'

'I certainly do not.'

'Thanks be to Jaysus,' says I. And, pulling out the plug, I cut her off.

Somehow management found out. In the Telephone Exchange you got a thing called an M.P.1.8., a sheet with the charge against you written down on it and you had to answer on that sheet. If they were pleased with the answer you gave, you could get a chief supervisor's warning. Or, if the offence was more grievous, you could get a secretary's warning. The most serious level was a minister's warning. I think I qualified for the minister's warning. Michael Kane helped me to compose a letter which was essentially my letter of resignation; they wouldn't have wanted me there after that.

From all the talk about Spain, I thought that would be a great place to head for and a few of us decided to go off to Spain. I don't know why: I think we were all kind of airy-fairy fellows really, we didn't want to work.

When I arrived home and announced that not only had I left my good pensionable job, but that I was emigrating to Spain, it was just too much for them. *'Oh, of course, that's you all over. You were always the same, even when you were going to school: the masters were wrong. You were always givin' out; you were never satisfied. Now you go and give up one of the best jobs in the country, and not alone that, but you're goin' away to Spain. Spain, I ask you. What you know about Spain? You don't know the language, you can't even speak English proper. And I believe the food is terrible in it – and it's foreign as well. If you have to go somewhere, why wouldn't you go to England, or America, where the people can at least understand you? But that would mean being normal like anybody else and that wouldn't suit you. Ah no! You'd always have to be contrary. Well, there's nothin' left for us now, only to pray for you and hope you don't meet your end out there.'*

Going to Spain was totally different from going to London. I had a very happy time down there. I went with Joe and I can't remember who else. We headed off with little or no money of course, through London and over to France and then on the train down through Spain. Four of us arrived in Seville and we hadn't a penny. We called into this little restaurant and the fellow running it agreed to give us a meal if we gave him our passports. So we gave him our passports and we had to go in there two or three times a week until we got a few bob together. And then we paid him off.

Two of the lads had already been out there and they told us how to go about getting a job. No matter what way you look at it, it was a scam. The idea was that you put an ad in the paper that read, 'Native English speakers will give private classes in English.' We couldn't have even tried to get jobs in any of the bona fide language institutes because we'd have been found out at once. So we targeted the poor unfortunates who believed what they read in the paper.

However, a few good things came out of this adventure. To carry out this scam successfully, it was necessary for me to peruse the English grammar, so that I might seem to know what I was at when I was giving them a lesson. As a result of all this perusing of grammar

by day, I learned how to speak English properly. By night, I learned a few things as well. While frequenting (for research purposes only) some of the more colourful bars of Seville, I learned quite a bit about the Spanish: Spanish wine, that is, Spanish ladies and, of course, Spanish music and songs and Spanish history. You wouldn't be speaking about Franco or anything political in case anybody would overhear you. I didn't know much about politics but I knew who Franco was.

We used to charge about a fiver a month for each class, but you could do a lot with a fiver a month out there in the late fifties. We eventually became locals at this sort of local pub, El Tres de Oro. We had a slate in that where we used to have our name up, *los irlandeses*. We'd all meet there in the evening time. I was very interested in flamenco so I had my guitar and I went for lessons to a man called Antonio Deosuno. He lived in these flats they had for working-class people. I used to go to him once a week or thereabouts. In the bar at night-time there'd be an old fellow who'd be playing the guitar and I'd learn things from him as well. And then on our own account I would be singing a few Irish songs as well. It was my first time to sing in public and I'd had no great ambition to play in public or go on stage or anything like that. I never have. I never could look forward, not because of any depressive thing but just because I was a person who lived for the moment. In one way that's a good thing but in another way it's not.

You wouldn't get near the Spanish women. You would never see a girl walking around on her own. They were very respectable and Catholic and would have a chaperone. Even if you saw a fellow who was going out with a girl, he'd be walking along and there would be a couple of women behind him, making sure they were up to nothing. And I never had anything much to do with the women out there at all. The women we met in the bar wouldn't be respectable.

We stayed in a pension that was run by a fellow called Manolo, a funny little man who walked a bit like Charlie Chaplin. He was always pleading with us for money and we would pretend at first we didn't understand him, but of course we knew we had to pay him. And we always paid him eventually, though we just mightn't always have had the funds the day he came looking for it. There were a lot of university students staying in his pension, students from the country, and we got

Ronnie (second from left) *in a bar in Seville, 1956. He had just got behind the bar and put on an apron as a joke for the camera.*

to know a good few of them. Myself and Joe Hackett pretended we were from a university here so we used to get into the university dining room. We used to have good fun in the dining room eating with the students. The food was simple – dishes made of chickpeas or stew and beans, there'd be no steak or anything like that – but nice food, I liked it. That was 1,500 pesetas a month – so three pupils for a month paid that bill.

I was giving a class to the daughter of a very wealthy household, Marie Luz. She was a lovely-looking girl but very stout. And she was young as well, only twenty-one or twenty-two. The lads were all saying to me she fancies you, why don't you marry her and then we'll all have a few bob. I don't think she was that way inclined at all, so it was wishful thinking on their parts. If I married her we'd be into wealth. Her family had houses in the country and houses near the sea and all that scene. I said, ah no, I'm not going to be caught that easy. She was a very nice girl but more interested in playing the guitar than she was learning English. So we used to play guitar as well.

I was very dark when I got any bit of sun so I looked sort of like a local. And I learned Spanish just by listening in the pubs. It was a poor part of Spain and not many people spoke English. So I ended up with a very good accent, but not really great Spanish. I enjoyed my time down there very much, but I never went native. I was always very careful about that, because we used to give fellows who went to England and came back with an English accent after a week a terrible time.

When we were down there we used to go to see all the big religious processions for Holy Week. They would carry big statues of Christ and Our Lady. This was the big week for the citizens of Seville, because in those days what tourists were around would come along to it. So it was a double-edged sword, it wasn't all religion. We were all good Catholics in those days and used to go to Mass. I wasn't a holy Joe, but I went to Mass on Sundays.

I went to a few bullfights and I thought they were great – to see these lovely movements. But then unfortunately the bull gets killed and has to be dragged out of the ring. The first time I saw it I got a bit of a shock. I didn't like that part of it. But at the same time I'm not going to pass judgements on a whole people's beliefs or core of beliefs. In Spain bullfighting is not reported in the sports pages; it's reported in the arts pages because it's regarded as an art. And it's been going on for such a long time. We couldn't go to that many bullfights because we couldn't afford it.

The first time we arrived there about October and stayed until the following June. And then in June all the big shots, the people getting the lessons, went on holiday. June, July and August, apart from being terribly hot, was a bad time for business for us. So when June would come it was time to be heading for the hills.

In the bar we used to go to, some prostitutes came in there every night. They used to come in there like working girls after a shift in a factory. And you wouldn't be so crass as to ask them about their work. Just take them at face value. We got to know some of them fairly well, and one night before we were going home there was a girl there called Juanita and she approached me and wanted to know if I'd like to go home with her. And I refused because I said it would be taking advantage and thanks very much and lovely of you to offer and so on. It caused a little bit of embarrassment. Eventually she turned around in one of these frocks that twirl up in the air and she spun around in it and she didn't have anything on underneath. So she just said, that's for everybody.

I left there one day with a guy called Kevin. Kevin was always a bit cleverer about money than the rest of us. He didn't frequent the pub as much as us. I can't remember which of the three summers it was, but I had very little money and we decided we'd hitch-hike all the way home. We went to the outskirts of Seville but hitch-hiking wasn't a big thing in Spain and we weren't getting any lifts. Kevin, who was ever the wise one, said he thought it would be better if we split up. In other words, I wouldn't be holding him back. I said, tell you what, whichever of us gets to Madrid first go to the youth hostel and we'll meet there.

In those days, in the days of Franco, members of the Guardia Civil, the police, walked between each village, one on each side of the road, all day. From one village to the next, and back again, and back again. All day. At certain times a lorry came along with more fellows to relieve the ones who had been out on patrol. It was said about them that they had to know somebody that knew how to read and write to get the job, so they were very much people of the soil and didn't have a lot of humour. People were afraid of them.

I was going along the road and I came to a place called Écija. It was a desolate sort of place where if somebody wanted to shoot you, nobody would ever find out. I met two of these civil guards. They asked me what was I doing and where was I going, and then they said what was I doing with a guitar and could I play it. I ended up playing them something. That seemed to pass by them. Then in the distance I saw another civil guard coming on the road on a white horse, one of the upper echelons. And then the lorry with the change of shift arrived simultaneously with him. So he quizzed me all over again about what I was doing. I said, I have to get back to Ireland and I'm heading to Madrid at the moment. After quizzing me for a while he told me to get in the lorry and they would drive me to the railway station in Córdoba. When we got there, he got a third-class ticket for me to go to Madrid.

That journey was a great experience because a lot of people brought on wine and cheese and everybody shared. Eventually I got to Madrid and made my way to the youth hostel. It was out in the outskirts of

Ronnie (second from left) *on the move in Spain in the late 1950s*

Madrid, so I don't know how I got there. I certainly didn't get a taxi or anything, so I must have walked. When I got there I passed by a window and sitting down tucking in was our friend Kevin. So I showed up and I don't know if he was all that glad to see me. I'd no money of course at all so he bought me something to eat. I said to Kevin later on that day, now tomorrow, Kevin, we're leaving at eight o'clock in the morning. 'Cause the next stop is San Sebastián. I woke up at seven in the morning and your man was not in the bed. So I put on my clothes and went out. And they were having an open-air Mass – it was Mass every day there – and there's Kevin, hands joined and kneeling down. I went over and I said to him, Kevin, we have to leave. He said, I'm at Mass, and I said, I don't give a fuck where you are, just get up out of there or I'll pull you out of it. Neither of us were great specimens to be getting into a fight. But we did eventually leave and got as far as San Sebastián.

Then of course we had to hitch-hike up through France. We hadn't any money at all, and one night we were after walking an awful long way and we stopped on the roadside where the grass had been cut. I said, we'll have to stay here tonight. He says, oh I can't sleep here, there'll be rats and everything. I said, it's either that or keep walking and we can't keep walking. So he copped a light in the near distance and we went over to investigate and it was a farmhouse. So I was for asking the man could we stay in the hay shed or something, but he invited us in and he gave us a glass of wine and fried eggs and bread and all that. It was nice and I was delighted to get it and he let us stay in the shed.

Eventually we got to the port where the boat was going to England. We were walking down towards the harbour, trying to figure out how we were going to get on the boat with no money. And we passed a house which said 'British Consul', so we decided we'd give it a lash. The man inside said he couldn't do anything for us because we were Irish. About three feet in front of the house were railings so we went outside and I said to Kevin, that's it. Kevin said, hold on a minute and he began to cry – he was able to turn on the tears – and he said in a loud voice how his mother was going to be dead and buried by the time he got home and he'd never see her again. All this was carried into the man through the window and eventually he came out and gave us fare.

Then we got as far as England and then we didn't have too much problem getting to Ireland. I forget how, but we might have bummed our way onto the boat or something. My grandmother of course lived in Dún Laoghaire, where the boat came in, so I said to Kevin, that's great, now we'll just go up to my grandmother's place and she'll give us something to eat. So we went up there and we got all the usual breakfast stuff, rashers and eggs and the whole thing. And we were delighted with ourselves.

Across the road from where my grandmother lived there had been a house of ill repute. Not ladies of the night, but families kept moving in and out, and it was let out in flats. The area was sort of quite nice and they tended to be a bit rougher than the ordinary. There were rumours going around that it was haunted and there was a Mass said in it. One of the last tenants in it had been an old man with a white beard. He used to sit in the top window just looking out all day. When my granny had fed us, I said, 'I see the old man is still across the road.' And she said, 'Not that old man: he died a year ago.' 'Well,' I said, 'I've just seen him.' I swear to this day that I saw him, but it could've been the hunger.

*

One of the summers I was home – in June of 1960, I think – an advertisement appeared in the *Irish Times* looking for a musician/singer to entertain guests in a hotel in Kerry after dinner. I answered this ad and received a reply in the affirmative, so I immediately set off hitch-hiking to Kerry. When I arrived in Killarney, I made a telephone call to the hotel, to be told that the boss would pick me up at the Laurels bar. It was there that I first met Ernie Evans, and so began what was to be a long association with Ernie and the Towers Hotel in Glenbeigh.

When Ernie and I arrived at the hotel, we had a few drinks and I sang a few songs, which he seemed to enjoy, and he was no mean singer of old songs himself. This first meeting began a friendship which was to last until his death. Not being at that time an habitué of hotels I didn't know what to expect. Ernie, though I did not know it when I got the job, was a master-chef, and while I was only, as it were, an employee, I dined in the dining room, where I partook of some of the finest food I have ever eaten.

The hotel catered mainly for what were called in those days the gentry of Ireland and England. These were people who stayed at the Towers for the fishing. Gillies were employed by the hotel to show these gentlemen and ladies where and how to catch salmon.

That summer turned out to be one of the most enjoyable periods I had ever had. Every evening after dinner the people would gather in an informal way in what was, I suppose, the residents' lounge, though it was more akin to a large comfortable drawing room. One of the regular contributors to these evenings was a man by the name of Marshall Hutson, who was a fine harpist and singer, but primarily a painter and, I believe, an associate of the Cork College of Art; many of his paintings and drawings adorned the walls of the hotel. The walls in every part of the hotel were covered with paintings, and among Ernie's collection were works by local artists, notably Maria Simmonds-Gooding, who lived on the Dingle Peninsula across the bay from Glenbeigh. Ernie was a great patron of artists, local or otherwise.

A completely different job I got one summer I was home from Spain was with my brother Gerry. Gerry, a carpenter by trade, was the foreman of a job which had been undertaken by a local builder. So I proposed that he should ask the boss if he needed any men. My brother, being very well aware of my lack of skill in any area of the building trade, was very dubious, but blood proved to be thicker than water, so he told the builder a few fairy tales and I got the start.

As luck would have it, the job was situated on the top of a hill, from where we could see the builder's yard, and as he had a red motor car we were able to observe his comings and goings at our ease: I was embarking on another fiddle, and, like all good fiddlers, I had to make sure that my bow was well rosined. From this vantage point we could tell when he was approaching our place of work, and on these occasions I would apply myself diligently to shovelling sand from one heap to another, or throwing planks and boards from here to there with such force and conviction that I had even convinced myself that I was a vital cog in the wheels of industry.

However, I was soon to be taken away from the comforting arm of my brother. Because when the boss next appeared on the site, he came up to me and said, I have another job in Killiney, and I want you to go there tomorrow. I was terrified but managed to conceal it. He then asked me if I knew anything about scaffolding, and I told him, without even blushing, that I had plenty of experience in this area.

Next day I arrived at the site in Killiney: it was a house newly refurbished and, even though not worth millions in those days, it was a very expensive-looking piece of accommodation. Scaffolding had been erected along the entire length of the front of the house, and it was a very long house. My job, it turned out, was to dismantle this scaffolding. This was a terrifying task, even to think about.

I managed to busy myself with bits and pieces until the boss had left, because naturally I didn't want him around the place while I was trying to figure out how in the name of God I was going to carry out his orders. When he left I climbed onto the scaffold and spent some time trying to figure out how to unravel this piece of Meccano. Things went well for a while, but then I interfered with some very important gadgetry. Says I to the other fellow that was working with me (and who thought I knew everything because I'd been away in England and Spain), 'Now don't ask any questions, Jimmy, just fucking jump.' So we jumped off and the whole thing came toppling down and ploughed into the lovely lawn. Needless to say, I was sacked out of that job.

*

The last year I was in Spain I met an English fellow one night and he said he was working on *Lawrence of Arabia* and it paid him about three times as much as teaching. I already had an Equity card from work I had done in Dublin in the Gate, so I went down to the place and showed it to them and they gave me a job – they kind of had to – and they dressed me up as a British Officer.

We were marching along this place, a sort of semi-desert outside of Seville. There were hills on either side of us and we were walking on the flat part. And I was in front of a whole square of fellows. We knew some of them from the pub because they would have been all or nearly all from the poorer-class people. This fellow from the production crew came over to me one day and told me to tell them to do something. I said, 'No, tell Johnny to do it 'cause he's the interpreter.' The official interpreter was getting paid more than we were getting paid. 'Anyway,' I said, 'I don't speak Spanish.' 'I heard you talking to those boys,' he said. 'Do you want to be here tomorrow?' 'I couldn't give a fuck whether I'm here tomorrow or not,' I said. By this time I had a few bob and I didn't care. I didn't have a great deal of money but maybe I had twenty or thirty quid, which was a lot of money those days when you could get a glass of wine for a peseta. So eventually I got pissed off and I said to them, 'Sit down,' and they all sat down. The next thing these Guardia Civil came galloping down on horses from both sides of the hills, waving long truncheons. So there was a scatter and that was the end of me and the film.

Patrick's Day came in the middle of it all and O'Toole invited anybody Irish to come along to this party. I went into a place where O'Toole was singing a song and I pointed out to him that he got it wrong. He said, 'You sing it.' So then I sang it. And then I sang a few more songs in the party. So O'Toole and me, we became temporary kind of buddies, buddies on the day. After that, I got invited to dinner one night and there were people there like Anthony Quayle and Jack Hawkins. One of them was sitting with a drink in front of him for ages and I said something like, 'Are you going to drink that fucking thing or not?' The waiter just got me and lifted me out of the seat. They knew what side their bread was buttered on.

That would have been near coming home time again, and that time wasn't so hassled because we managed to get a few bob from the film. And we got a bus from Seville to San Sebastián and hard work only started when we got into France.

Chapter 7

On one of my trips home from Spain I was at somebody's funeral. We all went back to the house on Collins Avenue and I was telling a few jokes and telling a few stories and I sang a song – the way it gets at a funeral. John Molloy was there and he straight away asked me would I go on the Gate Theatre with him. He used to do one-man shows there. Now I had no aspirations to go on the stage and I didn't know what to think. But I was kind of glad of the offer and so I said I'll try it out: it was another way of making a few bob.

I would sing a song while John was changing costumes. One time I played flamenco with another guy. Then he gave me my own little storytelling spot in the middle of the show, where I used to tell funny stories about people from Dún Laoghaire. I learned a lot from John Molloy, even basic things like don't turn your arse to the audience.

One night as I was leaving the theatre with John we ran into a man who John introduced as Hoddie. I don't think he was overly interested in what my name might be, because he addressed everybody as friend. Well, Dublin has always been famous for its Quare ones – or eccentrics – and it turned out that one of the best-known Quare ones was Hoddie, or George D. Hodnett, to give him his proper name.

We chatted for a while that night and John said to him, 'How is life treating you, Hoddie?'

'At the moment, friend, I am living in a disused coal hole in Waterloo Road and have been living there for some time. In other respects I have also been very lucky. Shortly after moving to my present abode I came across a gentleman who at a very reduced rate let me have a large quantity of canned foods, the only drawback being that they didn't have any labels. However, he assured me that they contained

SHAPES—A ONE-ACT EXPERIMENT

Grey .... **AIDEN GRENNELL**   Green ....

THE TH
by JOH

CAST
(in order of appearance)

Ned Doyle .... **JOHN MOLLOY**

Patrick Maher .... **AIDEN GRENNELL**

Young Jane .... **ELIZABETH DAVIS**

Mrs. Ryan .... **IRIS LAWLER**

First Undertaker .... **DES NEALON**

Second Undertaker .... **JOE O'DONNELL**

Third Undertaker .... **DERRY POWER**

Fourth Undertaker .... **RONNIE DREW**

The Fella with the Long Hair .... **DERRY POWER**

During both intervals Dublin street ballads will be sung by RONNIE DREW to his own accompaniment.

DIALOGUE & SHAPES — BY **JOHN KELLY**

DES NEALON   Red .... **DERRY POWER**

RD DAY

KELLY

The entire action of the play takes place in Ned Doyle's room, the two-per-front in a Mountjoy Square tenement.

ACT I: The First Day.

INTERVAL

ACT II: The Second Day.

INTERVAL

ACT III: The Third Day.

The play is directed by YVONNE VOIGT.

Settings by JOHN KELLY.

Bath by Hammond Lane Foundry Co. Ltd., of 111 Pearse St., Dublin. Table, Bed and Mattress by James Cluxton of 158 Parnell St., Dublin. Extra Stout by Arthur Guinness Son & Co. (Dublin) Ltd. Soup: Crosse & Blackwell (Ireland) Ltd., 205 Parnell St., Dublin.

NEXT PRODUCTION:

THE DALERS

By PADDY CULLEN.

only "the best" such as Irish Stew, Curried Chicken, Mulligatawny Soup, so I have for the last while been dining very well indeed.

'However, this morning I found I was down to my last can, and you may picture my chagrin when, on opening this last can, I found that it contained Stewed Rhubarb.'

Hoddie was a fine piano player and his consuming interest was jazz in all its branches. It was said that he had come of a wealthy family who lived in Blackrock, about five miles from the centre of Dublin. It was also said that Hoddie's father was a kindly man, who indulged his son's eccentricities and his passion for music, but when Hoddie announced that he was going to take up the trumpet, the father drew the line and informed Hoddie in very certain terms: *there will be no trumpet playing in this house.*

It was not an easy matter to deter Hoddie, and eventually he realized that an ideal location for his trumpet practice was practically on his doorstep: the beach between Blackrock and Sandymount, when the tide went out. This was the ideal spot and here he could practise without upsetting anybody, or indeed anybody upsetting him. Hoddie being Hoddie, it was of no consequence to him whether the tide was further out in the light of day or the dark of night. So, in the winter of 1943, he betook himself to the water's edge, his practice area, at three o'clock in the morning and proceeded to play his trumpet.

In a short time he was set upon by five or six policemen, who arrested him, and he was taken to Blackrock police station, where he was charged with signalling to German U-boats. It may have slipped their minds that submarines travel under water.

You know the way most people have a guru because they can't spell charlatan. Well, Quare ones or Quare hawks are so called because people can't spell chivalry.

After getting the start at the Gate, I then just continued on and there were places like the Coffee Kitchen in Molesworth Street, where anybody interested in folk music used to go on a particular night for a session. I met people there like Johnny Moynihan and Dave Smith and a whole lot of guys who are still at it. We were all young and really interested in it. And then of course there were certain purists as well who watched every line that was sung. They didn't go to the cafés and places we were hanging out. They would regard that as kind of rock and roll nearly.

Then John Molloy wanted to have this woman do a spot of Irish dancing. But he didn't want what was on the go at the time – the sexless kind of dancing that went on where the women were rigid. He wanted a girl with an ordinary frock on her, so that when she turned around you might see a bit of her leg. And he didn't want a céilí band either, so asked if I knew anybody who'd accompany a dancer. So I asked Barney McKenna. I knew him from the Fiddlers' Club in Church Street. Barney was a great banjo player. Still is. So he played for the girl. Then Barney and I used to go over to O'Donoghue's because John lived in Ely Place and we'd go over there to get paid on a Friday.

During that period, there was a regular session in the International Bar in Wicklow Street, and I went in there one night and I met Luke Kelly. He'd just come back from England. And he had an awful lot of songs that we hadn't heard, a lot of songs of social comment. I'd say, Luke, we're going to O'Donoghue's, and Luke would come with us and eventually he started going in there as a regular. So that was three of us. And then Ciarán Bourke was studying agriculture and the university was near by. So he used to call in and he played the whistle. We didn't consciously form, we just played. Ciarán spoke Irish very well and he was into it all, any area of Irish culture. Luke and myself were particularly interested in songs that had good words, good lyrics. I felt for the nature of the stuff we were doing that the lyrics were all important, which I believe still. A song is communicating with people. Entertainment is a different area. Well, you have to then work in some entertaining stuff as well; when you're on stage you can't just be wooden and you have to try and do something.

My interest in songs wasn't just singing for the sake of a knees-up. I got very seriously interested in Irish songs and music and I followed through the best I could, but I didn't regard it as a very intellectual pursuit. I just felt that I'd found a kind of niche that I fitted into. At last. After years of arsing around. My family still thought I was mad of course. Mad. *You're never going to get anywhere with a voice like that.* And in the ordinary way I don't suppose I would have but with the odd voice I managed to be able to put over certain songs, so that's how I got away with that.

Luke had the best voice if we're talking about a voice in isolation. But he also had a great presence about him. Barney has a sort of warmth and he plays the tunes excellently: he's unique also in the way he plays. I don't like to make statements about who I'm closest to of The Dubliners, but I would have great affection for Barney. As I had for Luke and Ciarán, but they're both dead now. Of course we were lucky to find John Sheahan, who was a great fiddle player.

After one of John Molloy's shows he took us out on the road and he called it a Ballad Tour of Ireland. This was before we had the name. We played in different places around the country. It was kind of a half-success. I remember in Enniscorthy we didn't have any place to stay. With whatever few bob we had we went down to the pub after the thing. The guy in the pub told us there was a big empty room upstairs but there was nothing in it. We said it would do us grand, we'd just lie down. We lay down on the floor, but as the night went on it got very cold. There was an old-fashioned carpet in the floor so we lifted it up and got in under it to try and get warm. You should have seen the colour of us the next morning. The dirt.

It was around the time that people around Ireland were starting to enjoy Irish music, though it took a while. In Germany people go see something new, to see what it's like. In Ireland people have to know what it's like before they go and see it, so we were up against that. They wouldn't have heard of this thing or know what we were all about.

I kind of knew Deirdre McCartan from around. The first time I really met her I was in the Gate. Her father, who was quite an old man at the time, had heard me singing on radio and he said he'd like to meet me. So Deirdre and another woman that I knew came up to the Pike and asked me would I go out to visit him at Greystones. He had quite a high profile and he had run to be president.

Deirdre and several other girls had taken over the Pike Theatre and they had a coffee shop opposite the theatre. And we used to go in there because you got seven and six a night or something for playing in there. One day we asked them could we rehearse there, one of the only rehearsals The Dubliners ever had. And so this thing came up about the Ronnie Drew Group because that's what people were calling

us then. I said, I don't particularly like the responsibility of my name being out front. So Luke was reading James Joyce's *Dubliners* and I said, why don't we call it The Dubliners? We did and that was it. That was it, the thing was done.

I came out to sing for her father and that's more or less how I started going around with Deirdre. It wasn't long before we got married. Her father died in March 1963 and we got married that August. Deirdre's mother totally disapproved. And I don't blame her. Here was I, a fellow going round singing a few songs, I wasn't likely to be able to provide a good livelihood. But I got very friendly with her after.

I didn't think much about what would be involved in getting married and the responsibilities of being married. I knew it was a serious undertaking but I didn't think far beyond that. I was looking forward to getting married, I wanted to marry Deirdre and that was it. We got married in Westland Row Church. Her mother didn't come to the wedding but her brother did. I didn't get the feeling that Deirdre was particularly upset about her mother, though maybe I wasn't as sensitive then as I am now. But I think she was philosophical about it. She was very sensible and very practical, and if she believed she was doing the right thing, that would have been it.

All my family were there. The reception was tea and sandwiches up in O'Donoghue's. Well drink and sandwiches. And there was a place around the corner called Mackey's Place, off Pembroke Street. And there were a lot of us living there in a little two-storey house and a gang of us bunked in there. After Deirdre and I got married we were going to Galway or somewhere but it was decided that we would have the house there when we came back. However, when we came back the locks had changed because they'd had a huge party the night we were married and unspeakable things were done and said, so the landlord had decided I'm not having this bunch around me any more. So then we had to get a place. First we got a bedsit in Baggot Street and then we got a flat in Waterloo Road and lived there for a couple of years. And then we went to Wellington Road. That was a lovely flat – three bedrooms and a lovely big living room. Cliodhna had come along before we moved to Wellington Road and Phelim was born while we were living there.

Deirdre was very strong and the great thing about her was she never, ever worried about money. Never, ever. And there were times down through her life when she had every cause to worry about money but didn't. And I never really worried about money either. We managed to get out of it.

When Lee Marvin sang a song called 'I Was Born Under a Wanderin' Star', one of the lines was about sights looking better looking back. Well, the best times for me in Dublin were from the mid-fifties to the latish sixties. One of the places John Molloy introduced me to was Groomes Hotel, directly opposite the Gate Theatre. Every night after the show it was over to Groomes (or even if there was no show). It was a great meeting place, and if you went there often enough you got to know everybody who worked in the theatre; the newspapers, painters, poets, writers and almost all visiting celebrities and a lot of other people besides.

Dublin at that time seemed to be a more compact place; it was easier to find people. We'll say, for example, you wanted to contact a particular person. You would call into Neary's, McDaid's, the Bailey, Kehoe's or Davy Byrnes (Groomes was strictly a night-time rendez-vous), and if you hadn't found who you were looking for by 2.30 you knew that the contents of all these pubs would empty into the back bar of Jammet's Restaurant. So in you went and there you would find the person you were looking for or someone who knew where he was. 'He's got a part in a play in London, and he won't be back for three weeks,' or whatever the story would be.

All this sort of thing went on for a good few years, until I got married, though this did not interrupt matters due to the fact that we rented a flat in Baggot Street. From the day I moved into Baggot Street, I became very friendly with a great character, known as the Brother. He was a driver of the Belvedere Ambulance, a very posh service based in Baggot Street. As he had, due to his job, very erratic hours, and I was doing mostly weekend gigs with The Dubliners, we used to go for great walks around Dublin. These walks were not taken in search of culture, but mainly because we didn't have a lot of readies. We often used to walk down to the Liffey, get the little ferry across to the Northside and ramble all over the place. We even went up to the top of Nelson's Pillar once. He was a good bit older than me and would tell me great stories about Dublin in his youth.

In those days, walking from Baggot Street through the Green to Grafton Street you could pass in the street, or run into in one of the pubs, the likes of Paddy Kavanagh, Seán Ó Faoláin, Flann O'Brien, Brendan Behan, Seán Ó Súilleabháin, Liam O'Flaherty, Jim Fitzgerald and many lesser known but equally loved people: Joey Betts, Wally the Coalman, Paddy the Van Driver, Mick Peters, Peter Mulligan, and so on, and they invariably had some good story to tell. Most of these people had a very genuine sense of humour and there's only a few of that sort left.

A friend of mine recently said to me, 'You know, Brendan Behan has a lot to answer for,' meaning, of course, his professional Dublin man imitators, the sort who accost citizens in street or pub, delivering what they imagine is the immortal one-liner, which usually turns out to be very mortal indeed.

One of the first gigs The Dubliners ever did was in O'Donoghue's and somebody asked us would we play in the Ashbourne House Hotel. We did and we got a few pound, a fiver or tenner or something, and then we went on, playing around Ireland. We used to play out in Howth every Saturday night in the Royal Hotel. Deirdre and Ciarán's wife, Jeanne, collected the money at the door so whatever came in, we got. Up to then we'd been getting a fiver or a tenner. Now we were getting a good few bob. And then we started doing a midnight concert in the Grafton Cinema, which was at the top of Grafton Street, and that was very successful as well. A short time after that Dominic Behan was in O'Donoghue's one day and he brought us up to the Embankment in Tallaght, so we played out there for a few years. That meant we had the Saturday night and the Monday night and the late-night show, so we were doing OK. We weren't making a fortune but there were no middlemen so whatever we earned, we kept.

Dominic Behan became a good friend of mine. I met Brendan a few times but I didn't know him all that well but I knew Paddy Kavanagh fairly well. I liked him, Paddy. A lot of people said he was this, that and the other but I liked him. When I was living in Pembroke Road we ran into one another in the pubs and around the place. He very seldom talked about poetry or anything. But then when you meet these people you're not actually taking notes. You're just with them getting on with it. He was eccentric. The funny thing is you remember the eccentrics and we forget those who called them eccentrics. And Paddy definitely, in any society, would have been regarded as an eccentric. He was never well dressed or anything and his shoes would be untied, and he'd go along the road muttering to himself. Then we'd run into Flann O'Brien but I didn't know him very well at all. He really struck me as grumpy. Then a lot of people thought Paddy was very grumpy, and he was, but Myles, as far as I was concerned, was grumpier.

Luke Kelly was with us for about a year when we started off, and then he decided he was going to go back to England to get some more material, but he was planning to come back. He was anxious to get more songs so he left for a year. At the time John Sheahan was in a duo with Bob Lynch and I asked the two of them to join us and fill in for the porter breaks in the Abbey Tavern and they did. When Luke came back, Bob left and John stayed with us. After Luke came back we made the first record. Nathan Joseph, who was a folkie from England, heard us and asked us to record. He had a record company called Transatlantic Records. It was The Dubliners with Luke Kelly and had Luke, Barney, Ciarán and myself.

Within the whole folk scene it was very exciting, but not among the mainstream audience. Amongst ourselves we were delighted to have made a record and felt very posh. Then we made about a record a year through the sixties. After the first record it was years of travelling around in old vans and buses. A fellow called John Sheridan managed us for a while. When we did a lot in the Royal Albert Hall we were being managed by Philip Solomon. Dominic had brought us to England to meet him and he got us a lot of work. And we played in those workmen's clubs up in the north of England and a lot of Irish and people of Irish extraction would come to see us. Then Noel Pearson managed us for a good while. I liked Noel a lot and still do. He got us good work.

I never really stopped to think about how we had ended up going from O'Donoghue's to the Royal Albert Hall in six or seven years. It never really affected me. I was just working away, and thanking God to be getting a few bob. It never got to me that we were as big as we were. I often wondered sometimes how we had so many people coming to see us, but I never got a big thrill out of it. I suppose I should have but I didn't. When 'Seven Drunken Nights' came out we were interviewed by BBC radio and they didn't like me at all because they kept saying to me: 'How does it feel to be on the *Top of the Pops?'* I'd say, 'It's great, we'll get more money for the gigs now.' And the interviewer kept on wanting me to say it's marvellous and so on. I said, by the way that song in no way reflects our talent. It's just a whimsical song that was played on the radio. People are very susceptible to advertising so they bought it. I'm under no illusions, but that's what happened, because it was a very whimsical little song. I still feel that. By some strange pattern it got into the top twenty. It was played on Radio Caroline, the pirate station anchored somewhere in the North Sea, so our stuff was being heard in Norway and Sweden and Denmark and Belgium and Holland and Germany. So then Germany opened up for us and we ended up touring quite a lot.

We went to America in 1968 and we were on the *Ed Sullivan Show.* It was OK but we did 'McAlpine's Fusiliers' and Americans couldn't identify with it. I think also the fact that we all had beards didn't make us very welcome in the place; Americans are very conservative. The Clancy Brothers were more clean-cut than us and we didn't have a twinkle in our eyes. We weren't like that at all. The only thing we'd do would be tell a funny anecdote now and again about somebody who had written a song like Brendan Behan or Paddy Kavanagh.

We did some songs like 'Fine Girl You Are' but when you're filling in a two-hour programme there has to be some in it like that. But we tried our best to keep to the stuff we liked, without being too serious. I think we presented the image that we weren't taking ourselves too seriously. I think that helped. Also, we were very informal.

People ask me what my favourite song is and I always say it depends on the humour I'm in on a particular day. I always liked 'Finnegan's Wake'. I got it listening to Dominic Behan. Then there was a lot of Dublin songs, like 'The Ragman's Ball' and a few more.

Before the Troubles it was valid to sing rebel songs, but in 1969 when the Troubles started I said I wasn't going to sing another rebel song in public. And I didn't. I don't think the others were quite united with me about not singing another rebel song, but I wasn't going to sing another one anyway, no matter what happened. I realized that little children and defenceless people were being killed. I've no problem with the IRA fighting the Brits, but when it comes to innocent people and children getting injured and hurt and killed, I wasn't going to add to it. Not that my contribution would have been greatly valued. But it was all I could do. We dropped a lot of the rebel stuff and there were piles of other songs which we did.

The Dubliners wasn't so much a band as a group of four or five individuals, who each did his own thing and was accompanied by the rest. I don't think we ever were a band as such. We never sang songs together nor rehearsed together. We just played together, that's all, and as we'd learn a song we'd introduce it into the set. Even for a big gig like the Royal Albert Hall, we'd more or less agreed in advance, 'We'll have the top lively, then quiet down in the middle and then at the end bring it up again.' That was about the size of it: there were no real rehearsals or anything.

Barney as far as I can see never suffered from nerves. I was terrible nervous about going on stage but I just had to live with it until I went on and then try to brazen it out. Once you got into the swing of it, the nerves went more or less. I don't know whether Luke was nervous or not, I never spoke to him about it. John looked after all the finances of The Dubliners and he paid any bills we had. He was kind of Minister for Finance. He had a slight tendency to be stern but it didn't get him very far because we just said, 'Ah come on, John.' There was one time Ciarán and I decided we'd give ourselves a wage every week and that way we'd save money. But on a tour in England we were after John: 'We're just not getting enough, John.' We needed money for food and everything like that. So John relented and we got extra money. And that night he came down to see myself and Ciarán sitting at the bar, drinking away. Food and gargle.

There wouldn't have been an awful lot of money, though somehow we managed to get a lot of drink down us. Professor Ivor Brown used to mind us. He was up in Grangegorman at the time and I occasionally had to go into him and be in for a day or two. You'd be drinking too much and you'd be sort of poisoned and the nerves would go a bit. He looked after a lot of us. Of course he would say that we shouldn't but I just kept going. I'd stay off it for a few months and then I'd go on the lash. You'd go in with the best of intentions to have just a few jars and go home, and three days later you'd still be on the lash. That happened far too often. Then you might go down the country and there'd be a bit of a party after the gig and it'd take you days to get home. I'm not proud of it, but it happened.

Of course Deirdre used to talk to me about it. She didn't drink at all but she loved the music scene, and I don't know how she did it, but she could ignore all the drinking most of the time. I see the seriousness of it and I don't know how Deirdre put up with me. But she did, I'm glad to say.

Cliodhna or Phelim have never said they hardly saw me, because I'd be off the drink for three months and in that period I would take them to the circus and take them to the zoo and take them everywhere. I had a fair amount of time at home as well. Then I'd break out one day and then I wouldn't be around for a while. I did probably the best that I could under the circumstances. But I'm not proud of it at all. You can look back sometimes and think that they were the good old days and great craic. But when somebody else is maybe suffering the backlash of it, you realize it wasn't all great craic.

We came to live in Greystones because Deirdre's mother was sick in St Vincent's Hospital and when she was getting better she came to stay with us. We had a big flat in Wellington Road. There was just Deirdre and her brother, so Deirdre was kind of looking after her while she was recuperating. Eventually the landlord was going to do a rent review on our flat, which meant we were going to have to pay more, so I suggested to Deirdre that since she was minding her mother anyway, and her mother's house was empty, that we move into it for the moment and look around for somewhere else to rent. Then this house came up and we bought it in the early seventies.

By then three of us had young children but it wasn't too tough because we were earning good money at the time. We never worked on a weekly or a monthly basis – just as money came in, we put it in the bank. Ciarán got a brain haemorrhage in 1974. We were playing in Eastbourne and he had to be brought to the hospital there. It was like a stroke and it was a terrible shock. After his treatment, Ciarán was left paralysed down one side, so he couldn't actually work again. Though we were shocked, I don't think any of us were morose kind of people at all, so we got on with it at the time.

In 1974 I felt my children were growing up and I wasn't seeing very much of them, so I decided to leave the group. I struggled through the next four years. I was doing things on my own but I wasn't doing great and I would've done anything that came along because I had to provide. I went back to The Dubliners at the beginning of 1979.

Chapter 8

In 1987 The Dubliners were in the process of making a CD to celebrate being in existence for twenty-five years. We would never have been a very organized group of people, so, as was our usual approach to such projects, we were more or less making it up as we went along, when someone, I think it was Eamonn Campbell, the guitar player with the band, suggested that we should maybe approach Shane MacGowan and The Pogues to see if they would be interested in joining forces with us, so that we could record a track together for inclusion on the CD. They agreed, and the song chosen was 'The Irish Rover', which had been very popular in the music hall era.

Now by certain zealots we would have been considered to have let the side down or to finally have become unforgivably 'blatantly commercial', and so on, and so on, for having chosen to record a song that was not traditional and, worse still, a song that had connections with the music halls. *Ochone agus ochone*. The truth of the matter is that I believe the folk police had given up on us years before.

Well, anyway, we recorded the song and we had a great time working on it, and part of the reason that we so enjoyed putting the track down was that the job was done in about two hours.

The CD was released fairly soon after that, and before we knew where we were 'The Irish Rover' was in the charts. As a result of this we (that is The Pogues and The Dubliners) were featured on the BBC's pop programme *Top of the Pops*. It finally got as far as number five or six or seven – I'm not sure which, but into the top ten. This of course meant we were being invited to appear on all sorts of television shows.

One of these TV shows was the *Tom O'Connor Show*, which had been scheduled for Derry on a particular Tuesday, and was to take place at lunchtime, which meant that the show would be finished at two o'clock in the day. Now this is a very dangerous time for musicians to be let loose on the public, particularly if they are of the breed that are known to have a fondness for unwinding after a performance with the aid of copious amounts of drink. In the normal run of things they're bad enough when they finish work at eleven o'clock at night, but at two o'clock in the day . . .

On the Sunday night prior to the TV show in Derry, The Dubliners were playing in Bandon in County Cork, so I decided that, instead of driving home to Dublin on Monday and then travelling to Derry the next day, I would travel from Bandon to Derry on Monday, a distance of about 300 miles, which, in Ireland in 1987, would have taken as long as a journey of 600 miles would take in any other European country.

Before I left on Monday morning, I telephoned Terry Woods, a musician with The Pogues, to have a chat about the forthcoming TV appearance, and during the course of our conversation I told him that I had not had a drink for about six weeks and that I intended to stay off it. Terry said that he was off it too. He explained that he would be travelling to Derry in The Pogues' bandwagon and, as he was off the drink, and as I was being a teetotal also, we would hardly want to be hanging around after the gig, and would I mind dropping him off at his home in Virginia, County Cavan, which was more or less on my way home. I, of course, agreed and said we would leave immediately after the show.

Having driven from 10 a.m. on Monday morning, I arrived at a town called Stranorlar in County Donegal at about four o'clock and decided that I had had enough and would book into a hotel for the night, and, since I wasn't drinking, I would go to bed early and drive to Derry at my ease next morning. The hotel I had decided to stay in was the kind of place where the ambience somehow suggested that frivolity or flippancy would be frowned upon, and if you had to speak, you should do so in a whisper. Also there didn't seem to be anybody else staying there. So I thought I would go out for a walk around the town. When I hit the street I looked up and down and there wasn't a sinner to be seen. I began to wonder had some plague or other visited the place and was it being kept secret; it was a very eerie feeling. Well, I bought a newspaper and made my way to a pub to have a cup of coffee and a read.

Inside the pub were four hoteliers from different parts of Donegal in whose hotels I had at one time or another performed. They had all the signs of four fellows on a day's skite and, as I knew them all, there were friendly shouts of 'What are you havin'?' I tried for a short time to insist that I would have coffee, but, being morally weak, I very soon quailed and joined the session.

Next morning I awoke at about 8 a.m. and, to my surprise, I wasn't feeling too bad. I was not well enough to face breakfast, so I just had some coffee, and then went to the reception desk to pay my bill, and was informed by some guests who were standing around that we had had a great night. That there had been piano-playing with many people doing their party pieces and I had contributed by singing and telling stories. Of course, I agreed that it had been a marvellous night – my agreement being a total lie because I couldn't remember any part of it. Not a very pleasant feeling, because somewhere deep down within yourself you realize that someday you will probably have to give it up completely. As they say in journalese, I made my excuses and left.

I arrived in Derry at about ten o'clock. After parking my car the first people I met were three lads from The Pogues, who were without a doubt suffering and from experience I knew they were badly in need of a drink. The problem was that the pubs would not be open until eleven o'clock.

At this stage I threw my hat at giving it up that day, and joined in the hunt for a friendly publican who might take pity on us and serve us with drink before opening time. The search was carried out by means of pushing gently at the door of every pub we passed in the vain hope that one of them might miraculously open. Eventually, after one of our polite nudges, a door did open and we went inside cautiously, to be met by two middle-aged ladies who were engaged in cleaning up the pub prior to opening time. They were very sorry, they said, but they were the cleaning ladies and would not have any authority to serve us with drinks. However, after some almost tearful pleading, their hearts melted and they thought it would be very unchristian to stand by and watch our suffering while the cure was so near at hand. So they broke all the rules and supplied us with a few drinks, which helped to steady us and to stop the shakes. We of course offered to pay for what we had consumed, but the ladies informed us that they were not allowed to go near the till and in any case didn't know how it worked. Before we left, we gave them a decent tip, and left enough money to more than cover the price of the drinks. We then made our way to the television studio.

We did several rehearsals and eventually the show was televised without a hitch, and we were free at ten minutes past two. At a quarter past two we found ourselves in a pub unwinding – in our case, a euphemism for getting locked. By this time Terry Woods threw in the towel and had joined us in our unwinding.

Before my memory deserted me for the second time in two days, I vaguely remember Barney McKenna saying that he would 'mind' Terry Woods and myself because we were very drunk and incapable, and that he would drive the car and book us into a hotel if necessary because he had only had five pints.

There was a problem, however. Barney had never driven an automatic car before and so he persisted in applying his foot to where, in a manually operated car, the clutch would have been. So that every time he went for the clutch, it was the brake he was hitting. The result was that while driving through the streets of Derry, he was hopping along like Rudolf Nureyev, only less gracefully.

The next thing I fully remember was being awake and looking at a dirty wall that was about six inches from my face. Around my shoulders was a grey blanket with holes in it, and I was lying on a narrow stretcher-like bed. My head, I thought, was about to burst; I was shaking, and feeling generally as though I might die. I sat up very carefully and turned my head to find myself face to face with Barney. I proceeded to attack him with all my hangover spleen.

'What sort of kip is this? Did you book us into a doss house or what?'

'Sing "The Auld Triangle" now, ya bollix,' Barney replied.

We were, of course, in jail.

I have fond memories of The Dubliners but I also feel a lot of it was run-of-the-mill stuff and part of me felt, and still feels, a sense of failure – that it became a bit like the civil service in the end. I've always considered myself a failure: I feel I've never done anything wholly right. I've always been nearly doing it but not quite getting there. But people have to live with no legs or some other sort of deformity, and if those things can be lived with then surely failure can be lived with. You have to accept it. Everybody will tell you, 'Oh no, how can you say that, because ten thousand people clap you on a night?' But part of that is reflex action and part of it is because you were reasonably good. But if you're great, that's a different thing.

I never felt that The Dubliners or myself did anything that was great. I often thought we did good performances and so on. But great? Never. I never thought great. We were well known up to a point, very well known in parts of Germany, Holland, Norway, Ireland and England, but that was what you'd call our beat. I felt we must have done good performances or they wouldn't have kept coming.

I'm not fully what I think I should be and I never have been. For example when I was in The Dubliners I didn't do enough work on the side, which would have made things better for me, and by extension for the whole group. That's one of the things. And then I feel I haven't done enough in that area of preparing things. Had I done so, I might have been more successful. I feel that that has contributed to my failure.

The Dubliners got the gig of playing at the first St Patrick's Day festival in London in 2002 and they asked me would I go with them. Deirdre and the whole family were there for it too. We were finished playing about six o'clock and we went off to the restaurant of this fellow, Richard Corrigan, and then there was a party dragging on and I got a pain in my arse from that. I heard there were a group of Irish guys playing in Ronnie Scott's, a group of about five of them. The actor Patrick Bergin was there and he came over and asked would I do something. I said, 'What am I going to do at a jazz club?' I sang 'Raglan Road' and Jimmy Faulkner accompanied me and the band came in in the middle and did a musical break.

It was terrific. There weren't many Irish there because this is a real jazz club and people from America who go to London automatically go there to play jazz. I felt as I was going through the song something was happening, and at the end of my little performance there was a kind of wait before they started the applause. And a big black man from New York, he just put out his hand – he didn't know me at all – and he said, 'Man, that was something else.' And that probably meant more to me than the Albert Hall or anything, because he didn't know me, he didn't know The Dubliners, and he didn't know anything about Ireland. That was the one time.

KINGSTOWN

'One of the nuns asked my grandmother to name the baby after a famous priest, Fr Ronald, so that's how he became Joseph Ronald.' – Cliodhna [In the thirties, Fr Ronald Knox, a convert from the Anglican Church, was a famous writer and broadcaster on religious matters and a writer of detective novels.]

Peg Maher

Paddy Drew

Dad's parents eloped. My grandmother told me that they were dancing partners and they used to win medals for ballroom dancing. Her family wanted her to marry somebody else. They made one attempt at eloping and that was foiled, but they managed it the second time. They had five children, Dad, Gerry, Tony, Joan and Margie.

Cliodhna, October 2008

Ronnie and Gerry

My grandmother was a seamstress and she made all their coats and things. His Aunt Eileen, that's what she did as well. There was a company called Brendella Skirts in Dublin at one time – my grandmother taught the woman who ran that how to sew. Dad always liked a nice suit and for years he used to get his suits from Joe Monaghan on the Green. He never found anybody who was quite as good.

Cliodhna, October 2008

The four Maher sisters in the 1970s: May, Eileen, Lal and Ronnie's mother, Peg

May, Lal and Eileen lived in the one house with their parents, where Dad was brought up, when he was growing up. May married Uncle Eddie after a seventeen-year engagement, Eileen never married, and Lal was a widow. Of the four of them only my grandmother had children, so they poured their love into their nieces and nephews. They really would have been like grannies to us as well. Auntie Eileen and Auntie Lal died within seventeen days of each other and I remember in work they weren't too impressed with me going off to another grand-aunt's funeral. I said, 'But she's like my granny, I have to go.'

Cliodhna, October 2008

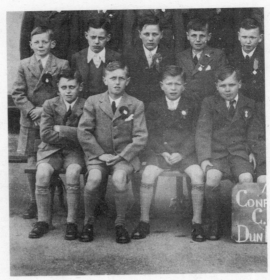

Ronnie's confirmation picture (he is front left). 'Dad looks different from the rest, as if he's saying, "Take the feckin' picture." He always had sunken-in eyes but it wasn't as obvious as he got older.' – Phelim

Ronnie in tennis whites. 'That would have been his grandfather and his grandmother sending him off to do the things that upwardly mobile boys should be doing. Today it would be rugby.' – Phelim

Living in Dún Laoghaire you felt cut off from the rest of Irish Dublin. You heard talk of Kingstown and the King as though he were our king.

Sunday Tribune, August 1988

I probably was sent down there [to his grandparents' house] out of the way or something when the next child came and then one thing led to another. I have certain good memories of it, but all in all it was a situation I'd have preferred not to have been in. When you're that age you accept what's there and you don't really question. You just go along with things. Then of course it just went on and it's only in later life that I began to question the whole thing.

Sunday Independent, February 1998

Joan Byrne [Ronnie's sister]: The story we always heard was that when Ronnie started school, we lived a mile and a half [away], there were no buses, we had to walk there and back and if it was raining or anything my grandmother would suggest: 'Let Ronnie stay here and he can go from here to school in the morning . . .' I think he [Paddy Drew] did have a major hang-up about Ronnie being kept by my grandmother: they sort of commandeered him and didn't allow him home. But what he really wanted was to be home with us.

September Song, RTÉ One, May 2008

My dad came from the school where this was a healthy thing, to think about things and to mull over them. In later years, when he started to focus on his upbringing, and the fact that he was brought up by his aunts and his grandparents, as opposed to living with his mother and father and sisters and brothers, he felt that this was something he had missed out on and that perhaps this added to this feeling of isolation or loneliness. I suppose when he would express these kinds of feelings he wouldn't necessarily be fielding for an opinion. Or a Band-Aid. So he wasn't really interested in you saying something like, 'Yeah, but Dad, do you not think that maybe you wouldn't be who you are if you hadn't had that upbringing? You wouldn't have the freedom of your mind in order to be able to make the choices that you made.' Dad

obviously had this idea that he wanted to do something with his life
and he wanted to do something special and make a difference.

Phelim, October 2008

My father was a carpenter and his big claim to fame was that he never
lost a day over drink even though he was fond of it. I mean he had a
good sup at the weekend. When I was born we lived in a tenement
but then moved to a council house in 1937, a very good, well-built
house – inside toilet, bath, ranger, copper cylinder . . . When I was
about three or four I moved to live with my grandparents. My grandfather had won thousands on the sweep and had bought a posh house
on Tivoli Terrace in Dún Laoghaire. I think the family thought they
would make a gentleman of me. Have me go to work in a suit. Maybe
not a doctor or a solicitor but certainly go to work in a suit.

Village, December 2006

I left school feeling I was a total idiot. There again, I don't blame the
teachers. The classes were so big. But I could never accept formulae
unless I knew what they meant and they hadn't the time to explain to
me. If people said that's the way you do it, I'd say why.

Sunday Independent, February 1998

I think the reason I wasn't good at mathematics was because I couldn't accept formulae without knowing exactly where they came from. And they would say, 'Well, that's the way you do it.' And I'd say, 'Yeah, but why?' I remember one question I asked in Algebra. They said, 'We'll say x equals pears and y equals apples,' and I said, 'Why not use what we know, pears and apples?' Looking back I think it was an intelligent question, for a child. I really didn't understand.

Interview with Theo Dorgan, *Invisible Thread*, RTÉ Lyric FM,
May 2001

I went to the Christian Brothers in Dún Laoghaire and that's the place where I had an awful lot of problems because I was looked upon as being a total dunce, which I probably was. I used to take all the blame myself at that time for being the dunce. I don't any more. In fact it was so bad that when we walked around the schoolyard at breaks, I was made to carry an abacus ball frame to show that I was bad at maths. I felt very humiliated and I would say it was the start of a bad inferiority complex. I'm not being dramatic but I just feel it was. I was there right up 'til sixth class and then I transferred to the secondary school and I only got as far as the Inter. Cert. I couldn't take any more of it and I got a reference from the [teacher] which, when you read between the lines, said, 'He is not exactly a criminal and doesn't mean any harm but I wouldn't give him a fuckin' job.'

Village, December 2006

I felt a sort of a loner, I felt not part of anything. See, I wasn't interested in sport. I never had any interest in any kind of sport. All I wanted to do was be out the country. I don't know what I wanted to do out the country, but I wanted to be out the country.

Sunday Independent, February 1998

Sheamus Smith [former classmate]: Ronnie was certainly by far the most intelligent person in the class, but probably the worst student in the class. He was different from the rest of us because he had a different attitude towards the teachers. He wasn't afraid of them as we were . . . We used to mitch from school and we used to go to Leopardstown Racecourse. Ronnie knew all the ropes. He was very

clever and streetwise. He just loved horses and he loved to watch the horses and the movement of them, even going down to the start. We'd be leaning over the rails and Ronnie would shout at the jockeys, 'Howya, head.' And the jockeys would always nod and I thought this guy is known by these jockeys but they were just being polite to two kids. But he had an abiding love of horses.

September Song, RTÉ One, May 2008

When you are a child, this is your world; how do you get over there. There was nobody with any imagination around. When I say that, people were caught up with getting on with life and they had no time, and I can understand it. I'm not laying blame.

Sunday Independent, February 1998

When I was a kid in Dún Laoghaire we used to go to a thing called the four-penny rush. We used to pay four pence on a Saturday morning. Between cowboy pictures and Laurel and Hardy, that was our whole diet of films. And I've never fallen out of love with Laurel and Hardy: I still enjoy their films. I saw them when they came to Dún Laoghaire, I think it was sometime in the 1950s. And they stayed in the Royal Marine Hotel, a place where the peasants wouldn't even venture into the front garden of, and I saw them walking down one day and I was thrilled. I've always loved them.

Playing Favourites, RTÉ Radio 1, February 2007

My great holidays every summer were to go to an aunt of my father's who had a little – what I called a farm: it wasn't obviously a farm; it was maybe ten acres and they had a cow – and her name was Aunt Jane. And we used to go down there near Clonsilla. Porterstown. It's about three or four miles the other side of the Phoenix Park. In those years – that was say 1944 – down there they used to grow strawberries and we used to help to pick the strawberries, which I didn't fancy. Even at that age it was back-breaking. Out there at that time there wasn't any electricity. We had to go to the well for water. And Aunt, Jane used to make the bread. Just the same as in the most remote parts of Ireland. And I loved it. And Uncle Dan was a great man to tell stories.

Interview with Theo Dorgan, *Invisible Thread*, RTÉ Lyric FM, May 2001

We'd go down there [to Clonsilla] for a few days. I used to love that. That was really heaven to me: my parents were there, my brothers were there, I was there. The whole ambience was one I wanted. I felt far away from Dún Laoghaire, where I was living, and I felt freer. I felt that I could go out and I could do things that I liked doing.

September Song, RTÉ One, May 2008

I didn't understand that you had to earn a living. I only ever wanted to be ridiculous things – like a jockey – never a plumber or a clerk. My father, who was a carpenter and came from a culture where hard work was everything, must have thought I was an awful embarrassment. But I never got the ramifications then.

Sunday Independent, February 2005

In the 1950s there weren't many music sessions being held in pubs or hotels, not like nowadays, but I remember there was a place called the Khyber Pass Hotel just outside of Dalkey – I'm not sure whether it wanted to be part of Killiney or part of Dalkey, whichever was the poshest – but they had music sessions there and very often a pal of mine and myself used to go there and from going there became friendly with a man called Val Browne and his wife Anne and when we got to know them well enough they invited us back to their house in Sandy-cove and he had a fantastic selection of jazz and blues records. I had heard jazz and blues before this period, but he really introduced me to the whole gamut of jazz and blues.

Playing Favourites, RTÉ Radio 1, February 2007

The problem about all these Irishy things was that they were terribly dowdy. The old Irish thing of s-e-x reared up. The women were almost strapped down in case anybody'd think they had breasts and they had lead at the end of their frocks in case anyone would catch a glimpse of knee.

Sunday Tribune, August 1988

I began dreaming about doing things. I'd been at a film, in the Adelphi or somewhere, and I saw a piece of genuine Spanish guitar-playing, and I immediately got interested in it. In those days there wasn't much money around but I eventually got down to it and I bought a guitar for a half-crown from some fella – I don't know where he got it. And we had to get strings for it and I started.

Interview with Theo Dorgan, *Invisible Thread*, RTÉ Lyric FM, May 2001

There were a great bunch of fellows there [in the Telephone Exchange] – Michael Kane, the artist, Joe Hackett, a poet, John Kelly, who later taught in the College of Art, many others. They opened up a whole new life for me because I had been living a life where there weren't any books. I used to go to the library myself and get books but I didn't know what to read, I had no direction.

Village, December 2006

All these thoughts I'd been having, whenever I'd mentioned them to anybody, they made me feel even odder than I felt already. But these fellas they just said, 'Hey, that's right, so what?' I was amazed. They

were a fantastic help. They said read such a thing and such a thing.
I'd never met anyone before who was seriously reading anything.

Sunday Tribune, August 1988

One night Ronnie was assisting a lady with an overseas call. When
the final connection was made, he was overheard to say, 'Now, mam,
will you please put in your twopence.' To which the puzzled lady
replied, 'Surely it must be more than that.' 'Ah no,' says Ronnie, 'you
see we have a sale on this week.' And promptly completed the call.
When reprimanded by his supervisor he simply replied, 'Sure you have
to do something to break the monotony the odd time.'

The Dubliners: 30 Years A-Greying Anniversary Tour,
UK programme notes, 1992

*Only in the days after Dad died did I read this account of the funeral
and it was from a man who claimed to have been a colleague of Dad's
in the Telephone Exchange and he said something about the famous
story about Dad talking to the wife of the Minister for Posts and
Telegraphs, and pulling the connection on her when he established
that she didn't know who he was, that that wasn't true and that that
in some way was an embellished story that Dad had sort of made up.
My dad was a storyteller and he loved the whole idea of embellishing
a story and over the years it became part of his stagecraft that if he
told a story, he would hone it. To me it's not really important whether
it's absolutely true or not: I have no doubt that something happened
along those lines. And he was as quick as a light, so he would have
had the presence of mind to say, 'Madam, do you know who I am?'
I absolutely believe it.*

Phelim, October 2008

We were all going around, discussing things into the early hours, and
we knew everything of course. But it's a very valid thing to do when
you're young. And then you can do it in a less excited way as you go
through life – you know, you can do your own bit of thinking, your
own bit of searching.

Interview with Marian Finucane, RTÉ Radio 1, December 2003

When I was young, nobody had any money anyway. It wasn't *Angela's Ashes* grinding poverty, but it was just the norm. There was no question of buying houses. Pensions? Hah! I remember meeting people who'd taken the permanent pensionable jobs after school and by forty-three or forty-four years of age, they were twisted and bitter. The way I looked at it was that you can't always wait for the green man to cross the road. Sometimes you have to go when it's red – to get to the other side.

Irish Times, April 2006

The honest outcast

Michael Kane

One day in 1956 I was seated at the switchboard of the Central Telephone Exchange, above the Post Office in St Andrew Street, when, in an idle moment, as the saying goes – which we weren't supposed to have – I was made aware of the entry into the switch room of a group of men, none of whom I had ever seen before. They were mostly young and had the accoutrements of our 'trade' – headphones, speakers and the dangling cable of a plug to be connected to the switchboard – hanging around their necks. They bore expressions of anxiety and oppression, and gave an image like a nineteenth-century engraving of a work-party of manacled prisoners. I wondered if that was the impression we all gave to anyone bothering to notice us in our collective glory. I realized they were a newly graduated class of T.M.N.T.s (temporary male night telephonists).

There was one in the group who didn't conform to the depressive image. He walked with the quick, dainty step of the true urbanite and wore a natty suit with razor-edged creases in the narrow trousers. He was wearing a tie. His walk was conspicuous, I realized, because he was wearing high-heeled, pointed boots. It was the era of the Teddy boy, but this was elegance of a different order. The boots were the key to their owner's enigma because I learned soon that he was a Hispanophile and a student of the Spanish guitar. His elegance there-fore was not one of the rather fusty versions pandered to in Grafton Street, which had been handed down by the British officer class and the 'city gent'. It was a more angular affair, sharp and metropolitan, giving a truly Mediterranean effect. I discovered he was a native of Dún Laoghaire and spoke in a kind of guttural that seemed to encompass the whole rich panoply of life and culture pullulating right round Dublin Bay. In personal conversation his speech was rapid and agitated, as if all his inner conflicts came up into his mouth when he spoke and fought over the words and themes like a cluster of demons. His name had a beautiful ring to it: Ronnie Drew.

He was rapidly assimilated into a group of fellow telephonists which, in the oppressive regimen of the public service, had become a kind of subversive, anarchic cell. The members shared certain interests and many prejudices. The prejudices were mainly to do with what we saw as the general imbecility of the world around us and especially the lunacy of the Telephone Exchange. The interests were the romance of art and, in a primitive kind of way, philosophy, metaphysical and moral.

Ronnie, because of the peculiar intensity of his numerous frustra-tions, turned out to be the most radical of us all, especially in terms of direct action. He was frequently issued with what were know as M.P.1.8.s, accusatory documents which would inquire, in what was in the circumstances a facetious manner, if perhaps you had used bad language on the line or otherwise abused a 'subscriber'. You might have been impolite to an irate caller driven to extremes of exasperation by the inadequacies of the telephonist, who was the first line of defence of the indefensible. Ronnie might be asked to explain a contretemps with a supervisor or some self-appointed authority figure on or off the lines or why he might have given short shift to someone who had failed to meet his high standards of courtesy and humanity. The exact words, naughty or otherwise, used by offenders would be quoted on the document, which led to many truly bizarre formulations.

On one memorable evening in the Exchange when, for some reason, tensions were high and nerves strained – supervisors, like slave-drivers lacking only the whip, stalking up and down behind our backs, urging us to 'Take them lights!' – Ronnie lost control. A particular super whose characteristic was a vigorous scratch every so often to the cleft of his buttocks – he became known as 'Goldfinger' – had an insidious whingeing way of finding fault with operators. On this evening, some snivelling rebuke of his was finally to exhaust Ronnie's patience and he flung off his headphones and stood out to confront Goldfinger on the switch-room floor, fists at the ready, threatening dire vengeance. The poor man cowered under a flood of supercharged vituperation. Ronnie was restrained and calmed with unexpected sensitivity by some of the more humane supervisors and given an enforced break, while Goldfinger was sent home to rehabilitate his *amour propre* and recover his nerve.

The following evening the inevitable M.P.1.8. was delivered, and Ronnie and I – who was deemed more experienced in matters of Exchange law – concocted between us as plausible an explanation of his behaviour as we could contrive, apologized to all concerned and heard no more about it.

Ronnie spoke in parables and maintained a passionate devotion to Christ the Prole. He cursed his tormentors – as we have seen – with livid bursts of invective. He loathed pretentiousness and all forms of fraudulence, especially the linguistic one that distorted the common sounds of speech in the interests of some farcical notion of gentility. He was incensed by those who pronounced 'party' to rhyme with 'shorty' or 'marriage' with 'porridge' but reserved an especial abhorrence for those who said, 'the lost time I was in Poris', which was not only a violation of language but a claim to a sophistication that the very phrase negated.

He was himself already fairly widely travelled and looked on the matter as a practical and direct way of acquiring knowledge – he abominated stereotyped views of foreign parts and their people – and not merely as something that was meant to impress friends and acquaintances. He hated tourism.

His ambition was to continue his lessons in Dublin with his tutor, a Spanish virtuoso of the guitar, and later go to Andalusia for more advanced study. He had a friend in Dún Laoghaire who was going to be a bullfighter.

In whatever spare time I had I sometimes visited with my girlfriend a kind of café-gallery called the Clog that was frequented by various forms of more or less artistic bohemian life. This included people of suburban provenance who practised versions of self-expression and informal 'creativity'. It was perhaps inevitable that some of these would be acquainted with Ronnie's tutor and his wife, a large lady of South Dublin origin who had translated herself into Spanish. It was probably through this nexus that Ronnie, my girlfriend and I were asked to a party in Foxrock at which this lady was to dance to the music of her husband's guitar. It appeared that Ronnie was also expected to contribute to the entertainment.

The nervous condition brought about by this prospect drove Ronnie to go at the cheese and biscuits and cheap Chianti with too great enthusiasm and too little time for its ingestion. The result was that he regurgitated the lot all over the dance floor while the enormous *danseuse* was undulating and pirouetting on it. It was a catastrophe. This is not the sort of thing the suburbs tolerate. Eccentricity is all very well and bohemianism warms the heart. One is liberal, broad-minded, tolerant, but this?! And in public *and* while the star performs!

I viewed it as an act of necessity, a frank asseveration of the truth consistent with Ronnie's metaphysic of Christ the honest outcast.

It was this insistent emphasis on 'honesty' that most characterized Ronnie and, principally through him, began to infiltrate the circle that had begun to form as a kind of counterculture to the one we were expected to adhere to in the Exchange, the College of Art and whatever other institutions – including the family – we were thought to belong to. We read Plato and made Socrates a hero. We read *The Catcher in the Rye* and delighted in Holden Caulfield's contempt for the 'phoney'. Dostoevsky would play his part, and Kavanagh in both his lyrics and his satires was grist to our mill. There was a kind of inchoate existential formulation in the air, a feeling of the need to grasp or create one's destiny and a definite conviction that it wasn't to be found in the Telephone Exchange.

There was an orientation towards Spain for various reasons, not one of which was political or ideological in any way. For romantics like us Spain was the flamenco companies that came regularly to the Olympia and the Gaiety, the plays and poems of Lorca, and some atavistic notion in the backs of our heads of a historical connection – as well, of course, as Ronnie's guitar and undigested evocations of Spanish landscape and life picked up in Hemingway's *For Whom the Bell Tolls*.

Ronnie set out sometime in the late summer of 1958. I followed in the autumn, hitch-hiking with a companion. We reached Madrid in early November and bluffed our way into becoming teachers of English in a language school.

I stayed till Christmas and was promised a job in Seville in the New Year. I arrived late on New Year's Eve and was brought to my pension by our friend Joe Hackett, who had left the Exchange earlier. The landlord, Manolo, let us in wearing a vest and pyjama trousers and slippers – it was two o'clock in the morning. We arrived in a long, dormitory-like room with four beds in a row. Despite the hour, the occupants of three of the beds were very much awake; Ronnie and his neighbour, Dave Power, were bickering mildly over some minor point of epistemology, while Bill Hall was serenely smoking. The fourth bed was mine.

Ronnie's guitar was part of the furniture of the room and was often employed to give background music and effects to farcical renditions of 'radio' plays. We adapted such classics as *Treasure Island*, whose protagonists would speak in grotesque parody of what we thought were West of England voices. They would be put through various absurd episodes of torment and abuse and dispatched brutally to stormy thrumming of strings.

Ronnie adapted well to expatriate life but found small failings to grumble about. He was fussy about his food, which surprised me, because we were perpetually hungry and I, at any rate, was prepared to gobble up anything put before me. He also found unsettling the habitual jeering of Spanish youths, who were unused to foreigners; he frequently had shouting matches with them in their dialect, which he had picked up through his remarkable musical ear. These altercations were made more dramatic when, after he had asked me to give him a haircut and I, having made a hames of it with a nail scissors, he went to the barber to have it fixed. The barber was unable to undo the damage and settled the matter by shaving off whatever hair was left. This, combined with the early stages of a first experimental beard, gave Ronnie, whose intensity of expression had a certain demonic dimension to begin with, the look of a convict escaped from *Les Misérables*. This was too much for the corner-boys and they excelled themselves in hysterical uproar. This, in turn, was too much for Ronnie, and his short fuse burned up rapidly. His rage was so melo-dramatic that the tormentors fled, one of them actually begging for mercy. They were convinced that this apparition was a genuine and dangerous lunatic.

Once, as Ronnie was coming back from an early morning private lesson, there seemed to be an unusual rumpus on the patio by the students who were our fellow lodgers. When he came in, he had an air of puzzled amusement and told me to make sure I had a look at the fellow who was painting the walls in the courtyard when I went out. I couldn't help noticing the painter when I did. He was a young man in conventional overalls but otherwise utterly unlike any house-painter I had ever laid eyes on. My discreet glance in his direction was met by a pair of astonishing dark eyes that seemed to sparkle with concupiscence. He had a kind of bouffant hairdo and a pair of but-tocks that would surpass most women's in curvaceousness.

When I came back to lunch, he had been integrated with the house-hold and was chatting with Ronnie and Dave on the patio surrounded by a chorus of students. Presently, with an air of great pride, he produced a collection of snapshots of himself in drag. He made a very attractive woman and enjoyed our amazement and the frantic wolf whistles and obscenities of the students.

I moved on at the end of February and didn't meet Ronnie again until September in Dublin. I was working for what became my first exhibition. Ronnie was at a loose end for a while. It was sometime during the next few months that he met the great mime John Molloy, a man of sinister charm and Mephistophelean appearance. This was a time when there was a curious and fortuitous coming-together of forces. Paddy O'Donoghue's pub in Merrion Row was opposite a small hall where student hops were held. The College of Art was five minutes away, the College of Science round the corner, Trinity and UCD ten minutes' walk, the College of Surgeons across the Green. Molloy lived in a mews off Ely Place. Representatives of all these institutions, ex-students like myself, the denizens of the dance hall as well as Molloy and various actors who might be working with him congregated in the pub. Ronnie and I were regulars. Molloy suggested that Ronnie play his guitar in one of the reviews he produced at the Gate and tell a few of the stories he entertained his friends with. This was not just the beginning of Ronnie's theatrical career, it was the very inception of the Folk Revival in Dublin. Molloy organized a folk concert in the Hibernian Hotel that included Ronnie, who had been inspired by the work of Dominic Behan and the Dublin ballads popularized by his brother Brendan and others. His voice was ideal for the transmission of these songs. Barney McKenna, Luke Kelly and Ciarán Bourke became habitués of Paddy's and, more or less by accident, The Dubliners group was formed.

Ronnie and I saw each other frequently in those years, either in one or other of our homes, which were near each other in the Baggot Street area – I have a memory of a brief period when he lived next door in Waterloo Road – or in O'Donoghue's or a local for a drink. He was reading Dostoevsky's *The Idiot* at one stage, the 'hero' of which we both identified with. Between that and whatever other books were doing the rounds we had plenty to talk about. He was a hugely moral man but not of the small-town variety that confined itself to sexuality. He was something of an anarchist in politics and hadn't much time for politicians. His music brought him into contact with all the great practitioners of the folk tradition throughout the country and he developed a great love for them and their unaffected genius, which transmitted the soul of ancient culture. He absorbed this culture both in his music and his personal life and gave it back to us

John Behan, artist, Michael Kane and Ronnie, 2004

transformed and enriched with a metropolitan ingredient and made the humorous side of it his own.

In Ronnie's case the existential dilemma was handled in a truly heroic spirit. The troubled metaphysician of 1956 was still grappling more than fifty years on with the complications of a life to be lived decently in a tragic world. His devotion to Christ the proletarian outsider never wavered, understood in a spirit of self-sacrifice and generosity and compassion for his fellow humans. He gave away more than he ever kept for himself.

He was a wonderful singer with a wondrous presence, a unique delivery and a feeling for the collective values of his songs. His is a true voice of the people, for the people, especially those most in need of the cheering balm of great, popular music. Long may his voice endure.

The picture on page 87 shows Ronnie outside the GPO, O'Connell Street, c. 1950.

PART 2

Dubliners

John Molloy's company for The Real Molloy *in November 1961: John Molloy on top; below him, Sheila Donald* (left) *and Dolly MacMahon* (right); *and below them, Ernesto Aragon, flamenco guitarist* (left), *and Ronnie*

After a funeral one night I was in a house and I was telling these stories. And I was terribly shy when I was young. I couldn't relate to anyone. And I began telling these stories about my grandmother going to funerals, and [John] Molloy was there and he was breaking his heart laughing. I first thought everybody was laughing at me and then I found out that they were laughing at the story. So Molloy asked me would I go in the Gate Theatre with him. I'd never been on stage in my life. John used to do these one-man shows and a lot of characters he played and he would change clothes and in between his changing clothes I would sing a song. And I really got to love it. I loved what he did – telling stories and all – and I still love it.

Rattlebag, RTÉ Radio 1, September 2004

Ronnie (right) *in a Gate production with John Molloy, Des Nealon and Iris Lawlor*

I was influenced by people like Maggie Barry. Maggie was one of the great old – for want of a better word – street singers. I remember being at fairs and hearing these ballad singers: literally ballad singers – they would sell the sheets. I saw the last of them. I'd lived in Dún Laoghaire. I didn't have a sense of being Irish. It was a strange place, Dún Laoghaire. There were people who used to put Union Jacks over the wireless in them days when the queen'd be making a speech. A lot of them had had husbands who were killed in the Dardanelles or somewhere. So I never had a sense of being Irish. It was only when I started moving around that I got to feel it. And then I heard people like Dominic Behan singing and then I met people around singing and I loved all this and I was very interested in the history of the songs and what they were about.

Rattlebag, RTÉ Radio 1, September 2004

Performing at the Gate with Barney McKenna and Mary Jordan on spoons.
Mary's mother, Peggy Jordan, ran the Pipers' Club on Thomas Street and
was a key figure in the folk movement in Dublin at this time.

I began to realize that we had a heritage of our own here and that
took me to the Church Street Club, and the Pipers' Club on Thomas
Street. From then on I got very interested in traditional music and
began to go to Fleadh Ceoil, before they became very popular.

Hot Press, December 1986

Even as a very young man [Barney] was one of the best traditional
players you could come across. Yet, just because he had a Teddy boy
hairstyle, he wasn't allowed into one of the traditional Irish music
clubs in Dublin. That's how narrow the whole thing was.

Irish Examiner, March 2005

I'm a Dublin man. I sing Dublin songs the way I learned them, the way I think they should be sung. You don't expect me to sing as if I were from the Aran Islands, do you?

Gaelic Weekly, Christmas 1965

A lot of people involved in traditional music at that point in history thought that only certain instruments could be played. You had to look dowdy. I think we helped, in that we presented the music as being a bit of crack, as well as just playing. I picked up songs in Kerry, and I heard the same songs from guys in Donegal. We just picked up a bit here and a bit there, whatever suited us. I was as Irish as anyone living in the Aran Islands, but there was no point me imitating a Galway *sean nós* singer.

Hot Press, December 1986

Y'know, I promoted the first ballad concert in Dublin. We held it in the Hibernian and it was so full a couple of hundred had to be turned away. I was thrilled, artistically. I thought I'd be great to have a concert every month or two! But next thing I knew some fellow was asking me to appear at a ballad concert in the Grafton Cinema and I did it as I needed the readies.

Our first booking as a group – we were known as the Ronnie Drew

SENSATIONAL ATTRACTION

And the showband that is going to cause a great sensation in the Irish and English Dancing World in the immediate future.

EVERGLADES

SUN., 12th JULY, 1964

RONNIE DREW Ballet Group

MRS. LAWLOR'S BALLROOM NAAS

ADM. 7/6 :-: 10 p.m.—3 a.m.

Group then – was in O'Donoghue's pub. They were a great help to us when we were starting. We used to ask Paddy, 'Can we sing a song?' We'd arrange to meet the Clancys there and the ballad thing built up.

Spotlight, May 1967

Ronnie and the boys were young lads playing for free drinks at O'Donoghue's pub where Peggy [Jordan] found them. Peggy got them to work and didn't pay them with pints of porter. She was the very first impresario in Ireland to pay traditional musicians. People thought this was a dirty thing, turning the traditional music into a business. Peggy Jordan started the whole music scene at the Abbey Tavern in Howth, later established the Embankment in Tallaght as a venue, followed by her tremendously popular midnight music gigs in the Grafton Cinema Dublin.

Dubliners Magazine, 1997

Ronnie was the warm-up act when Micheál MacLíammóir performed his show about the life of Oscar Wilde in the Embankment. Embankment-owner Mick McCarthy persuaded MacLíammóir to venture out of the city by reminding him that in his day Oscar had taken his show to America's Wild West.

[Luke] came into O'Donoghue's pub in Baggot Street. He had a forceful and friendly personality and when he began to sing I loved his singing . . . Luke was the type of character you could not ignore. He had great integrity and stood up for what he believed in.

Entertainer, September 1985

The first gig with Luke arose from O'Donoghue's. Barney used to join Luke and me there and then Ciarán Bourke, who was an agricultural student in university, he used to come in. In those days you had to seek permission to play a tune. I think it was around about Christmas one time Barney and I said to Paddy O'Donoghue could we play a tune and from that day to this we never stopped playing.

Village, December 2006

City people in those days, they were seeing a lot of *fillums,* and they wanted to be a sort of Mickey Dazzler – an old-fashioned phrase but they wanted to be modern and with it – and I think they saw Irish music as representing the older Ireland that they didn't want to associate with, all Paddy-the-Irishman stuff. They felt that they were more – I suppose the word would be 'hip' today – and they kind of rejected it without giving it a good hearing. They were more into the ballroom dancing and all that. See we'd two fine musicians, John Sheahan and Barney McKenna, and they played jigs and reels but came out on the stage: they were two Dublin fellas, beardy, a bit dishevelled, were known not to be on any great quest for respectability, and known or at least perceived to be guys who didn't give a damn very much. Which was fairly true. We didn't go out to be unconventional but at the same time we rejected all ideas of respectability for respectability's sake. I think it may have introduced a lot of people who hadn't given Irish music a good listening to and people who may have come to hear us may have moved on and got a far deeper interest in Irish music.

Interview with Alan Corcoran, *Ireland Tonight*, RTÉ Radio 1,
February 1997

Eamonn Campbell clearly remembers what it was like seeing The Dubliners for the first time. 'I just couldn't believe it. I was somebody who'd decided he didn't like Irish music, but this was something I'd not heard before, there was a whole new aura about the lads.'

Folk Roots, March 1993

We just wanted to get across the fact that the music was still alive, that it had never died. In England and America they'd had a folk revival, but in Ireland it was there all the time so we didn't need to revive it. There was a certain amount of fanaticism about it and the thing was regarded as sacred. That attitude divorced a lot of younger people from being interested in Irish music. I think we helped to take it out of that. We didn't set out to do that, but the fact that we were obviously enjoying playing it so much transferred itself – we proved you don't have to be an academic to enjoy Irish music.

Folk Roots, March 1993

Their 'We do it our way, to hell with the rules' attitude informed everyone in Irish music that followed, from Phil Lynott to Bono to Shane MacGowan.

BP Fallon, The Best of Ronnie Drew, sleeve notes, 2007

They were the original rebels. People think of the people who broke the mould as being the children of the sixties – the Dylans and the Rolling Stones and the Beatles. I've always felt that it was actually the generation of people who were in their twenties and early thirties in the fifties who actually were the real rebels – the Burtons and the O'Tooles and the Harrises. And then you've got The Dubliners and they're all of a similar generation, breaking the straitjacket of convention at a time when at a certain age you got a job for life and you stuck with that and you had a family and you got a terraced house. And I know an awful lot of people looked at their lifestyle at the time and thought, 'God, this is outrageous.'

Phelim, October 2008

Billy Connolly first came across The Dubliners in Glasgow City Hall in the sixties: I had never seen such a collection of hairy people in my life. I had never seen such energy, honest to God energy, like Luke Kelly's. I had never heard a voice as extraordinary as Ronnie Drew's.

I had never heard banjo-playing as amazing as Barney McKenna's. Ciarán Bourke looked like the gypsy from one of his own songs who was quite likely to run off with your girlfriend if you didn't keep an eye on him. If my memory serves me well there was also a little guy called John who did the most beautiful version on mandolin of 'Roísín Dubh', which I will remember until my dying day, and with a bit of luck will have it played on that occasion ... folk music's Rolling Stones.

The Dubliners: 30 Years A-Greying Anniversary Tour,

UK programme notes, 1992

There were all these stories about Ciarán. Dad used to say about Ciarán, if they were going on the piss together, 'You start on Monday and I'll meet you on Wednesday.' He would drink pints just for thirst. Whiskey he drank to get drunk. Ciarán and Luke, they really took it to another level and so they were an accident waiting to happen, really. They were wild.

Ciarán had the constitution of an ox. He was huge and had a huge appetite. Mam had made this big pot of stew for anybody who'd fallen by the wayside, if they wanted to come back and restore themselves with this pot of stew and have a sleep. But Mam came back this time and Ciarán had come back to the house in the meantime and was lying on the couch in the sitting room, fast asleep, with the empty pot of stew beside him. He'd eaten the entire thing.

Phelim, October 2008

The thing about The Dubliners is – line 'em up, the hardest rock 'n' roll bands in the world, AC/DC, Led Zeppelin, The Who, Oasis, Nirvana, U2 – we're all a bunch of girls next to The Dubliners.

Bono, *The Late Late Show*, RTÉ One, February 2008

My dad had always been a bit of a hypochondriac. He said he was sitting in O'Donoghue's and it was something like eleven o'clock in the morning and he was reading one of the morning papers and I think it must have been an English paper because there was an ad in it for some new pill for morning sickness and he was reading this and he turned around to somebody like Peter Mulready, a regular in O'Donoghue's, and said, 'Jaysus, Peter, I think I have this thing here; it looks like exactly the right thing for me.' And Peter says, 'Ah for fuck's sake, Ronnie, put that down, that's for pregnant women.' He didn't associate morning sickness with being alcoholic. He didn't even think that he was an alcoholic because at the time men working in Guinness', and even fellows working on sites, they'd have maybe two or three pints at lunchtime, they'd have three or four pints after work, then they'd go home and they'd have the dinner and they'd go back and they'd have another four or five or six. They'd never get mouldy.

Phelim, October 2008

There wasn't the social stigma about drinking then that there is now. I mean, drink was accepted in that when you came to a certain age, you drank. Drinking was never looked upon as actually wrong. People would refer to someone who was drinking a lot as, 'Ah sure, he's fond of a few jars – he's a harmless poor ol' divil. The worst he does is make a fool of himself.' Once you didn't do anything too stupid, making a fool of yourself was OK.

Hot Press, June 1992

Mam wanted to act. She went to college and dropped out before her final year and then she joined the Pike. She never talked much about growing up. Her father was a member of the IRB during the Rising and became a member of the first Dáil and later ran for the presidency. Her father would have been sixty when she was born but she never considered him old. In fact, she would have considered her mother the older one. She never talked about meeting Dad and didn't go in for reminiscing.

Cliodhna, October 2008

Padraig McCartan: My father had died the previous March 23rd in 1963. My mother was alarmed all right at this minstrel, as she used to call him. It wasn't that he was a minstrel so much as he didn't come from the land and therefore he wasn't of any substance and couldn't be counted as good enough for my mother's daughter.

Tonight with Vincent Browne, RTÉ Radio 1, June 2007

Padraig McCartan: Deirdre fell madly in love with Ronnie the minute she saw him. She adored the ground he walked on . . . She [Mrs McCartan] refused to come to the wedding because she didn't approve of the union. She believed that this minstrel would never be able to keep Deirdre in the style to which she felt Deirdre should be accustomed.

September Song, RTÉ One, May 2008

By the time I came along my grandmother was happy enough and she and Dad became great pals. The story goes that Ciarán came out to collect her when I was born and they disappeared on the beer.

Cliodhna, October 2008

We got married in 1963 and it's a mystery to me how she put up with me. I'd say it's a total mystery to her too.

Sunday Independent, February 2005

Deirdre's father, Dr Patrick McCartan (left), *with Seán McBride*

Deirdre's mother, Elizabeth, here with her son, Padraig McCartan, 1967

Barney McKenna and Luke Kelly serenade the bride and groom outside
Westland Row Church, August 1963

(front) *Bridesmaid Betty O'Shaughnessy; Deirdre and Ronnie; Barney*
McKenna; Luke Kelly. (back) *Deirdre's brother, Padraig McCartan; Ronnie's*
aunt Frances; Ronnie's father, Paddy; Ronnie's aunt Eileen; Ronnie's brother,
Gerry; Ronnie's mother, Peg; unidentified priest; Ronnie's sister, Margie;
Fr Michael Cleary; Ronnie's sister-in-law, Ursula; Ciarán Bourke

Paddy and Maureen O'Donoghue gave us the back bar and we had a great party. There wasn't any wedding cake, but we had plenty of sandwiches and tea and later we had the loan of a house off Pembroke Road and Paddy O'Donoghue sent around a few barrels.

Evening Herald, August 1988

They went to Galway for a night and wherever they stayed in Galway they had to show a picture of themselves from the paper to prove they were married.

Cliodhna, October 2008

We lived in a bedsit in Baggot Street until we saw a ghost. Then we moved out. Then we got posher and we moved to Waterloo Road. And then we got even posher again and moved to Wellington Road. We had a good life and I have no regrets.

Tonight with Vincent Browne, RTÉ Radio 1, June 2007

The Dubliners first came to UK notice at the 1963 Edinburgh Festival. There they met the head of Transatlantic Records, Nathan Joseph, and started their recording, and UK broadcasting, careers.

John Sheahan: We tried to have this meeting to talk about the future of the group. We got together in the pub and there was a little bit of discussion about gigs in the future and so on and I was trying to decide whether to give up the job or not. During the course of the evening everyone got drunker and drunker and then a row broke out between Barney and Ronnie and the next thing I knew the group was breaking up before my very eyes – it was all, 'Fuck you, fuck you, you can play on your own.' And that was it, the group had split, and I was thinking I was glad I still had my job and I was mad to have got involved with that crazy lot in the first place. Then I get the phone call from Ronnie the next day. 'You OK for Friday?' I said, 'But the group broke up last night!' And he said, 'Oh, for fuck's sake, don't take any notice of that, it happens every week!' So I said fair enough and quit my job.

Folk Roots, March 1993

Sean nós *singer Joe Heaney lived with the Drews for six months in Wellington Road. When he moved out, piper Seámus Ennis moved in. The picture shows Joe Heaney with Ronnie and baby Cliodhna in O'Donoghue's with fellow musician Al O'Donnell in the background.*

Ciarán Bourke's wedding to Jeanne Bonham in April 1964. He and Barney got their hair cut under duress only after Ciarán's father prevailed upon Maureen O'Donoghue to use her influence. 'She marched them off to the barber's and nearly stood over them while the scissors snipped. She had threatened to bar them from the pub if the deed wasn't completed to her satisfaction,' Ciarán's sister Eileen wrote for the 1998 Dubliners Magazine.

At the Sheahans' new house: Mary Sheahan with baby Siobhán, Ronnie,
Deirdre and Cliodhna, and John

We had a manager once who suggested we all bind ourselves together
formally with a contract and this solicitor drew up this long-winded
bloody thing and we all pulled away from it. If you want to split up,
you're gonna split up whatever you signed, aren't you? So we've never
had a formal agreement from that day to this and I believe that's
partly why we've stayed together. A commitment to bind to each
other is an ingredient for breaking up really.

Folk Roots, March 1993

Nelson's head, from the top of the recently destroyed Nelson's Pillar, was
revealed when the curtains opened on The Dubliners' Gate show, Finnegan
Wakes, *in April 1966*

On the recording of the show [*Finnegan Wakes*] Ronnie had some lively exchanges with the audience. There is the odd revolutionary suggestion too, i.e. that all the books by Irish authors which are banned in Ireland should be written in the Irish language. This, so Ronnie said, would be the greatest incentive for the Irish people to learn their own language.

The Dubliners Scrapbook: An Intimate Journal, Mary Hardy, 1978
(in 1967 Mary Hardy started the first Dubliners' Fan Club in the UK)

I met a man at a funeral a few months ago. He was telling me that in the mid-sixties he had a boat on the Shannon. He said, 'I came across

Ronnie giving an interview with Deirdre and Cliodhna, 1966

Danny Cummins, Ronnie, Cecil Sheridan and Dubliners manager John Sheridan. John Sheridan was the group's first manager, a man full of sensible advice, such as 'Remember, lads, no stopping for a drink till we get past Inchicore,' and sound philosophy, 'Never pay all your bills and leave yourself short.' 'Dad always used to quote him and say, "That's a great bit of philosophy."' – Phelim

your dad and he was wandering around and he didn't have any money on him and he was on the piss. Obviously he'd done a gig somewhere down around there and ended up on the piss and spending all his money. Of course, your dad was as mad as a mongoose in those days.' They took him onto the boat and the only berth on the boat was at the bow and Dad had to sleep in the shape of an S-hook at the front of the boat and he was giving out – not at all appreciative of the hospitality. They got to the next town, where there was a train station that would bring him back up to Dublin. They pulled in and they all got off the boat and they walked him up to the railway station. And when Dad walked past the ticket office one of them naively said, 'Ronnie, you've just passed the ticket office.' And Dad said, 'Ah fuck the ticket office.' And he climbed over the railings and there was a train in the station on the platform and he just walked right up to the top of the train, had a few words with the engine-driver, hopped into the engine and off they went. There was no question of buying a ticket or this is going to be a problem or anything.

Phelim, October 2008

Ciarán MacMathúna: There was one memorable journey to New-castle West in County Limerick for a fleadh with the group. I was staying in a hotel but the lads hadn't booked in anywhere. Instead they slept in crates under a stage for Irish dancing in the middle of the town square, and I remember Ronnie and Ciarán waking up next morning to find themselves surrounded by cattle, it being a fair day. I think it took about three or four days to get back. Travelling with The Dubliners, it usually took about three or four hours to travel to some part of the country, and three or four days to get back.

Irish Times, May 1988

In the beginning there was a lot of drinking all right. But, as the years go on, you have to taper off. At first you're euphoric, you're young and it's all great. As it goes on, you still enjoy it – I don't think I'll ever give it up – but in a quieter way. You don't notice people being screwed up by it when you're in your twenties and thirties, but it starts hitting fellows in their late thirties and forties. You can do it when you're younger. We were just having a fantastic time.

Hot Press, December 1986

Paddy [Kavanagh] would talk about horse-racing and all that and he wasn't at all kind of academic. I think he left that to the would-be literary people. The actual literary people who were knocking around weren't all that kind of hand-on-forehead, thinking hard. They were all out drinking and carrying on and having a bit of crack and Paddy was great. Like his shoes'd be half off him and he'd be untidy and he'd be shouting and spitting and drinking whiskey by the dozens in McDaid's.

Interview with Alan Corcoran, *Ireland Tonight*, RTÉ Radio 1,
February 1997

I remember one time we were in McDaid's. Paddy was taking bicarbonate of soda with whiskey for his stomach and some posh gent came in and said, 'Paddy, if you continue to take whiskey with bicarbonate of soda, you'll ruin your tummy.' Paddy replied, 'I don't mind fornication, it's kind of natural, I don't mind the man robbing to feed his family, in certain cases I'd even condone murder, but I hate vulgarity. The word is "belly" or "stomach".' I loved that. I thought it was lovely, the thing about that is that you can't forget. It so hits the nail on the head.

Village, December 2006

In the mid-sixties Ronnie Drew and Patrick Kavanagh fell out for a time. Ronnie explained the row in his one-man show: see Part 5.

We used to pass one another on Baggot Street Bridge. We'd walk by without speaking, like a pair of children. One day on the bridge Patrick said to me, 'Have a drink.' I said OK, might as well. That was Paddy's way of forgetting the whole incident. I said, 'Will we go into Mooney's?' Paddy said, 'No, I can't go in there. I'm barred out of it, we'll have to go to Searson's.' I said, 'Paddy, we can't go to Searson's. I'm barred out of it. We'll have to go to the Clubhouse.' 'Oh no,' he said, 'we'll have to go to Andy Ryan's because I'm barred out of the Clubhouse.' Well sure I was barred out of Andy Ryan's. We just said, Good luck, see you again sometime. But I never saw him alive again.

Hot Press, December 1986

Mary Kenny: One point for St Patrick's Day about Irish music: only the Irish can bear it for long . . . These past two summers in Dublin have been ballad-crazed. The best ballad bard of all, I think, is Ronnie Drew with his group The Dubliners. They sing proper old bawdy Dublin songs with a proper sawdust Dublin accent. Although The Dubliners are well appreciated in their native city and equally beloved in Belfast, I don't know if they are exportable. You see, they are the real thing.

Guardian, March 1965

An early family holiday in Spain. Deirdre was frightened of birds, which explains her position in the top picture.

Yet it was 1967 which was The Dubliners' *annus mirabilis*. Now signed to the Major Minor label, owned by the Irish entrepreneur Phil Solomon, whose other discoveries included The Bachelors and Van Morrison, the group recorded an old ballad, 'Seven Drunken Nights'. With Drew singing the incomparable lead vocal, it was released as a single and banned by the Irish national station RTÉ for its bawdy content. The offshore pirate station Radio Caroline had no such qualms and played it heavily. It was no coincidence that Solomon was a director of the radio station and the regularity with which his disc jockeys played the record had the desired effect. The record made the British top ten in May 1967 and The Dubliners appeared on *Top of the Pops* alongside Jimi Hendrix, The Kinks and The Who.

The Times, August 2008

When Dominic Behan introduced us to Philip Solomon everything changed. He sold us as an international folk group and it worked. We were soon booked for more television, more tours abroad and success at the Albert Hall.

Entertainer, September 1985

It's an age-old story and it's not meant to be a social comment or anything of that nature. It's just meant to be a bit of crack, a bit of fun. Of course, in 1967, Ireland, or parts of it, was still living in the fifties, or maybe in the thirties, when you couldn't mention such things as s-e-x. You couldn't say it. You could maybe spell it but you certainly couldn't say it. The bishops even – that they should give their time to giving out about a bunch of fellas! The fella in Cork, Lucey, he got up and said it from the pulpit, using words like 'lewd' – a bloody bit of an auld ribald song. I wouldn't go so far as to say ribald; it was just vaguely kind of risqué. And then they banned it on Radio Éireann. I thought that was the funniest thing of all time. And I'm nearly sure Joe Heaney sang it in Gaelic on Radio Éireann before that. I think anybody who was responsible at the time in Radio Éireann would probably laugh as well and say, 'Weren't we terrible gobshites!'

Interview with Alan Corcoran, *Ireland Tonight*, RTÉ Radio 1, February 1997

Terry Wogan: Speaking personally, and without trying to denigrate in any way The Dubliners' success, I can't for the life of me understand how this record has become a hit. As someone who has always been a big fan of The Dubliners, and Ronnie Drew in particular, 'Seven Drunken Nights' seem to me way below their best work. Their performance is fair enough without being outstanding, but the song itself is repetitious, monotonous and, after about a minute and a half, frankly boring. It lacks the usual Dubliners fire and brio and certainly doesn't compare with their outstanding recordings of, say, 'McAlpine's Fusiliers' or 'Finnegan's Wake'.

RTÉ Guide, April 1967

Damien Dempsey: Ronnie was singing 'Finnegan's Wake' and it was like hearing Jimi Hendrix for the first time. It was so raw and passionate and belligerent. It was an amazing experience. And in that year The Dubliners had 'Seven Drunken Nights' on *Top of the Pops* and Jimi Hendrix was on with 'Purple Haze' and he actually said he thought Irish music was very funky 'cause he heard The Dubliners.

The Late Late Show, RTÉ One, February 2008

The Dubliners are a truthful group. I sing some songs I collected ten years ago. How do I get them? Well, you won't find them in a dance hall or in a lounge bar in Galway. You talk to some old fellow and say, 'Give us a song.' He might sing 'When Irish Eyes are Smiling', but the next one might be good. Oh, and Colm Ó Lochlainn books – I get songs from him. I don't know if The Dubliners are a ballad group or folk group or what. A ballad singer is one man, on his own. There are all these tags nowadays – 'happenings', 'psychedelic', and so on. I'm not sure of the proper name for what we're doing. Ah, what the hell. What does it matter? We like what we're doing and that's what counts.

Spotlight, May 1967

'Seven Drunken Nights' was recorded in three minutes and sold 40,000 copies within two days.

John Sheahan: I remember when we got into *Top of the Pops*, we met some other showband fellas in London. It was during Lent when the

Luke and Ronnie with BP Fallon. 'He's a real gentle guy. My dad always really liked people who were just really gentle. He didn't have much time for people who were really brash.' – Phelim

bands used to go over there – there was no dancing here during Lent in those days. And one of the lads said to Ronnie, 'You're in the charts, you know.' And Ronnie's reaction was, 'Is that good or bad?'

The Late Late Show, RTÉ One, February 2008

It is no ambition of mine to be part of a pop industry. I don't want my individuality to be taken away by any success.

Time, October 1967

In our contract with Phil Solomon we had a special clause put in that gives us the right to turn down unsuitable work – that means any work we don't want to do. He can't force us to do something we don't want – we'd just turn around and say, 'We're sorry. You can sue us.' No, artistically we're quite free . . . It's not as if our hit has saved us from starvation or anything. In the last four years we have never – and I mean *never* – played to an empty seat. We've even managed that in the middle of a bus strike.

Spotlight, May 1967

Joe Heaney [talking about 'Seven Drunken Nights']: I learned all my songs from my father and all of them could be sung before children. There is nothing wrong with 'The Days of the Week Song', or 'Seven Drunken Nights', as it's called. It is well known in Irish as 'Peigín agus Peadar'. You'll find the story in international folklore about a man having to go away to work for a farmer for twenty years and coming home to find a whiskered youth on his bed. It's really his own son whom he has never seen.

Evening Herald, April 1967

Joe Heaney emigrated to the United States in May 1967, just as the song he had given Ronnie was a hit. 'I did not like to have to make the decision to leave Ireland permanently, but there just is not a living for me as a folk singer here,' he said just before leaving.

Seámus Ennis and Joe Heaney were shamefully treated by the government, shamefully treated. They're too interested in looking after all the successful people. And Seámus Ennis and Joe Heaney were very successful men. They didn't get the rewards for it but they were very successful in that they did very well what they set out to do. Success is a very arbitrary kind of term because people presume that because somebody gets a million pounds for it, they're successful. It doesn't necessarily follow at all.

Sunday Independent, February 1998

Ciarán Bourke: I like to feel – so do Ronnie, Barney, Luke and John – that when we sing ballads and play Irish traditional music we are encouraging people to know more of their country and thus to love it. You can have your pop and your fine orchestrations, which tend to kill natural expression. But give me and the rest of the boys the basic material that has remained practically unchanged down the centuries.

Spotlight, April 1967

The Dubliners had another big UK hit with 'The Black Velvet Band', which was released in August 1967, shortly after which they commenced a huge all-England tour that started in the Royal Albert Hall.

[Barney] hadn't arrived in London, and we were all there, fretting and rehearsing and wondering would he turn up at all. Finally, with the place buzzing and five minutes before we went on stage, a taxi arrived from Heathrow, and out hopped Barney with his banjo. We were all demanding to know what had delayed him when the taxi driver interrupted to say, 'You're lucky we got here at all – all he knew was that he was playing in a big roundy place near the park!'

Sunday Press, March 1987

An immortal, if unprinted, quote from a recent Ronnie Drew interview went something like: 'There's three great questions. What is life? What is art? And where the fuck is Barney McKenna?'

Irish Times, August 1992

Completely out of character with the record charts they continually find themselves in, they do not conform in any way, they retain their rugged personalities, all have beards and careless hair, open-necked shirts with rolled-up sleeves. In no way could they be described as 'with it', their Irish brogue is harsh but pleasing, and their manner, casual, warm and friendly but professional.

Ronnie is the eldest of The Dubliners at thirty-three, and is permanently surprised to find himself in the pop world. He is happily married, loves children, has black hair and beard, and the most photogenic pair of blue eyes ever.

Luke Kelly is twenty-six years old with a halo of wiry ginger hair. He grew up in Dublin's dockside. He left school at thirteen and a half and went through the usual gamut of jobs, starting to sing folk songs after realizing they were not as square as he had been led to believe ... Some of his likes are good-quality casual clothes, Beethoven, violin concertos, reading and staying up late, as well, of course, as 'good black stout'. But he says, 'Everything fascinates me.'

Barney McKenna is considered to be one of the world's greatest banjo players. He became interested in music at the age of six. He clearly remembers breaking the strings of his Uncle Jim's mandolin, his Uncle Barney's fiddle, and even blowing his father's melodeon out of tune. All the family played a musical instrument of some kind. At twelve years of age he tried to join the Number One Army Band, but was thrown out because his vision was not up to scratch. By this time he had mastered the banjo so well that he embarrassed most musicians who had ever attempted to play it.

John is very precise and quiet. He is the only member of the group who drinks nothing stronger than Coca-Cola.

Ciarán is the only Dubliner with a university education, and this he tries to live down. He is a great dreamer and hates to live in the city ... He is deeply involved in literature and the origins of music and would be content to sit up all night quietly telling stories and reciting poetry, if suitably fortified.

Programme notes for 1968 UK tour

Mam used to say about Ciarán that he really loved being in a band. In a way for Luke and Dad and even John and Barney it was a sort of a means to exercise their talents, but Ciarán loved being in the band. And he also apparently used to absolutely adore meetings about contracts and things like that. He loved all that. Percentages and stuff. He was a very intelligent man.

Phelim, October 2008

In July 1968 The Dubliners topped the bill at the Royal Albert Hall again, where they were introduced by Dominic Behan as 'the only group capable of performing Irish music with guts'.

If ever a group made folk popular in the contemporary sense, it is The Dubliners, who have had the widest possible success with the least concessions to commercial pressure. Their performance last night sang all the cold gloom and unresponsiveness out of that vast barn and entirely transformed an otherwise uncertain evening.

Maurice Rosenbaum, *Daily Telegraph*, 1968

What they lack in sophistication, The Dubliners more than make up for in musicianship and charm. . . . Ronnie Drew maintained a running slanging match with the hecklers who seem to haunt this particular group.

Financial Times, 1968

From the side of the stage that night I watched them. It was pandemonium. There was no barrier between audience and performers. They were shouting at each other, abusing each other.

'Luke, give us the "Fol de diddle rye" wan,' someone in the audience was shouting.

'You,' shouts Ronnie, 'would ye try to have manners. I mean I know ya weren't brought up with them, but would ya try.'

'Give us "Finnegan's Wake", Ronnie.'

'I'm only getting paid to be up here,' says Ronnie. 'D'ya mind if I sing me own song? Do ya mind? Barney, give us your E.'

[After having sung "Twas down by Christ Church'] 'That's a great song,' Ronnie tells the audience. 'That was banned by Radio Éireann. They said it was dirty. They didn't ban Elvis Presley, though, from singing "Baby, let's play house". 'Cause he's famous he couldn't be singing anything dirty.'

Ronnie needs no excuse for a tirade on hypocrisy.

Liam Clancy, *The Dubliners in Concert*, sleeve notes, 1965

Five full-bearded, raucous, archetypal Irishmen are one of the few groups that can lift an audience . . . Their appeal lies in their complete Irishness. They switch from abandon, often bawdy ebullience, to maudlin sentiment.

Financial Times, July 1969

Rasputin looks like Peek-a-boo when he's compared to Ronnie Drew.

From *The Dubliners Live at the Albert Hall*, sleeve notes, 1969

With his bushy black beard and mournful pale blue eyes and the most fantastic voice in the whole western world of folk, he is hardly anyone's idea of a glamour boy.

The Dubliners Scrapbook: An Intimate Journal, Mary Hardy, 1978

The beard came about for two reasons. I was with John Molloy of the Gate Theatre and I got a lot of warts on my face. Now the doctor told me not to shave and by the time the warts had gone away again I had a beard and inquiries were coming for the fella with the beard. So I figured it was an economic fucking necessity to keep it there. And it may also be that I don't have a face like Rock Hudson, you know.

Village, December 2006

I was always reasonably well dressed in those days. I'd always wear a suit. Generally I'd have decent trousers and a nice shirt. Americans didn't know what to make of the beards and the long hair. Relatively speaking my hair was long. The hippies were protesting at the time and right-wing people were criticizing their image. But there we were, with beards, long hair and *suits*. Generally, people who wear suits shave and polish their shoes and have short back and sides. There was a lot of confusion . . . I find you can fight people better if you're as coherent and articulate as they are, and if you're dressed even better than they are.

Hot Press, December 1986

You know what I think of hippies? Well, I believe that they're off their heads for a start. Let them take their drugs if they want as long as they don't take them up around my place. This flower thing is a passing craze. Another form of exhibitionism, like the beatnik cult. Pay no attention to them and they'll forget about it.

Spotlight, 1969

Five bearded songsters from Dublin were imprisoned in a storeroom at the rear of a church social hall for nearly an hour while a milling throng of admirers – as many male as female – battled for autographs and adopted devious ruses – such as hiding in the men's room – to get a name on a piece of paper or a 'How're ya, ma'am?' from Ronnie Drew and his associates, Luke Kelly, Ciarán Bourke, Barney McKenna and John Sheahan. The group had played a two-and-a-half-hour show reminiscent of a lively ballad session back home at the Embankment or the Old Shieling.

Evening Herald, October 1969

*'This picture was taken in San Francisco. Hippies hadn't arrived
here yet so it was really a photograph in order to take your man in the
background.' – Cliodhna*

*In October 1969 Ronnie was made an honorary member of New
York's mounted police. He had to don a uniform, mount a horse and
be escorted down Broadway by a police car with sirens screaming.*

I'm no golfer and I hate gardening. Give me a horse and let me go
galloping around the Sugar Load near Greystones. That's what I like.

Sunday Press, November 1968

Phelim: My mother was a very steady influence and didn't take much
nonsense. She was an exceptionally warm woman but there would be
times when she would maybe withdraw that warmth if she was angry
and you would know all about it.

September Song, RTÉ One, May 2008

Padraig McCartan: I wouldn't describe Ronnie as a person suffering
from depression in the depressive sense. I suppose I, among others,

*Ronnie learned to ride when he worked in the Towers Hotel in Glenbeigh.
This picture was taken on the strand at Glenbeigh in the early 1960s. In
1969 Bacardi, the horse he bought from the Towers Hotel's manager, Ernie
Evans, won first prize in its class at the Dublin Horse Show. A few years
later he had to sell it to settle a tax bill.*

Ronnie, Deirdre and Luke on a pitch-and-putt course, probably on the way back from a gig. Luke was into golf, but Ronnie took it up only late in life.

Ronnie, Deirdre and Cliodhna at the Spring Show in 1967

would say, Ah, sure he's coming out the other end of one of his drinking escapades. But certainly he would go into himself and become very introvert for days on end maybe ... His way of handling the silent treatment was to get up and to go out and he would go down to the Curragh. He would stay down there and ride out with them until lunchtime, wander back to the house looking the picture of health, fresh-skinned, freshly tanned, bright-eyed, and in the whole of his health, not looking at all like he had been on the tear the previous night. And Deirdre used to say, 'Look at that bloody fellow.'

September Song, RTÉ One, May 2008

When The Dubliners started, our reputation was well earned because we drank a hell of a lot. We didn't have any other social outlet. We played, then we had a few drinks. And when we'd have a few days off, we'd drink some more. There were parties every bloody night of the week. And parties meant bringing drink to places and drinking it. Or you'd go to afterhours pubs. Or up to a place on Capel Street where you could get wine, given to you in teacups poured out of a teapot. Sure drink was everywhere in those days – you couldn't avoid it.

Hot Press, June 1992

Luke: We have an image of being devil-may-care, unpredictable, hard-drinking artisans. We're not really. Of course, we drink, but it's not our complete way of life. Entertaining comes first and when we're booked for a show, we turn up in time – sober. John Sheahan doesn't touch the stuff at all . . . Another thing, singing in pubs is not our real forte. We're gradually getting away from it. A two-hour concert is what we relish. No noisy drinkers or interruptions from popping corks or clanging trays. I don't think it's a bad idea, though, having a raucous sort of image. You know, the tough Dubliners!

Spotlight, April 1967

I remember asking him about his drinking and how much he drank and all that. And even on a day when he wouldn't be drinking he would have a couple of gin and tonics for breakfast. The first one made him gawk a bit. Maybe the second one. But then by the third one he kind of found his equilibrium and then he would drink on and off, then throughout the day. This might not be a day when there was a session involved. It was just a regular day.

Phelim, October 2008

We had fantastic times and we had a name for drinking which was, I suppose, earned, but at the same time we didn't have the money to be drunk all the time. We never took any drugs. We didn't know about them, to be quite honest; maybe if we'd known about them we'd have had a go, but we didn't know about them at all. It was kind of the thing you did: you played music and you drank.

Interview with Alan Corcoran, *Ireland Tonight*, RTÉ Radio 1, February 1997

He got sick in about 1970. Very, very sick. He spent some time in John of God's. He'd been into John of God's a couple of times

'Dad's dying in that picture. You can see it. And I think Luke is as well. You can always tell when Dad's dying because he'll have the hair plastered down with water and he looks like he's in bits.' – Phelim

throughout his life. He used to joke about it almost, 'Going into the big house.' I think he did get very sick and that was a blessing in disguise because it cut his drinking. Throughout our upbringing he would go for periods of time where he didn't drink. I don't remember those periods being very long. If he went ten or twelve weeks without a drink that would be the longest. And then he would go on a binge for a couple of days. Basically what he would do was he would drink himself to the point where he couldn't drink any more and then he would need to get some medical assistance and then that would get him back on track. But there was always that thing, even during the sober period. And he suffered from depression as well, there's no doubt – and that, mixed with the feeling of wanting a drink but not allowing himself to have one – white-knuckle sobriety, I suppose – played havoc with his emotions.

Phelim, October 2008

Some people grow up at twenty-one, others at twenty-five, but I'm afraid I didn't really grow up until I was thirty-six. When I got married at twenty-nine, I was a bit of an eejit – not for getting married, but for the way I behaved. Both of us treated life as one big party.

Irish Independent, October 1974

My dad was more of a worrier, but my mother always just firmly believed that money would come from somewhere, and it always seemed to. She didn't have expensive tastes. She would spend money on clothes and if they were going out for dinner they would always get the bill – no matter who was there, and everybody was welcome. In my teens if I had friends who happened to be around they would always be invited to whatever we were doing. My mother had a real way of just paying the bills. But then there'd be periods in between, say, if my dad was away, when she'd literally be at home all the time. She wouldn't be going out. She wouldn't be going for dinners. She wouldn't be going out to meet friends in nightclubs. So, I think she always felt when there was a reason to celebrate, spend the money and really enjoy it.

Phelim, October 2008

Deirdre – never ever in her life, never ever do I remember her worrying about money. She liked having money, like us all, but she never worried about it. She always said, ah something will turn up. And she never got on to me. She never said, 'You better get out and get a few gigs.' Never ever. And something always did turn up.

Tonight with Vincent Browne, RTÉ Radio 1, June 2007

I think the precariousness of the business probably changed him to an extent because obviously he was a man with a young family, a provider. If there was a lack of gigs, then he'd get worried. But I think in his youth he was pretty fearless.

Phelim, October 2008

Phelim: I think back now . . . of my father being away, six or seven times a year, maybe more, for two to three weeks at a time sometimes. The older I got, the shorter the tours got, I think, as the lads began to

'They never danced. Dad would sometimes do it but Mam really didn't like it.' – Cliodhna

realize it was taking such a toll on their lives, being away from home so much. Initially the tours would be four or five weeks and I remember one tour seven weeks to Australia and that sort of thing. And it was a conscious decision that they were reluctant to exploit any financial rewards that might be garnered from going to America, because they just felt that it was just too far, for too long and would disrupt family life too much. My mother was remarkably strong during those periods. She just accepted that that's what my dad did and that's how the money was made and that's the sacrifice you had to make.

Arts Show, RTÉ Radio 1, May 2008

Cliodhna: Mam made it very easy for us. She made it very normal for us. Because it was a very unusual life in that Dad would be away six or eight weeks at a time and then when he'd come home there'd be a sort of party and out to the Shelbourne for lunch and bags full of presents and going here, there and everywhere. She kept it very normal and on an even keel.

Tonight with Vincent Browne, RTÉ Radio 1, June 2007

Cliodhna in an Austrian-style dress brought home from one of Ronnie's tours. Phelim got lederhosen – but they were confined to the dressing-up box.

When they came home we would all go out to the airport to meet them. Mam always brought us out to meet him. And then there would be a big lunch in the Shelbourne. I remember one day I went into school with a note for the teacher: 'I'm sorry Cliodhna hasn't done her homework – her father came home last night.'

Cliodhna, October 2008

I'm very fond of John. I would sort of look on John and Barney as uncles in a way. And Luke and Ciarán. They were like an extension of the family. John's kids and us used to get together at these things. And there is always a nice feeling when we get together with the Bourkes too. There's a kind of a common bond there. You don't have to explain yourself. You see each other and you're totally accepting of each other.

Phelim, October 2008

Michael D. Higgins [on the memories of his wife, Sabina, of her friends Deirdre McCartan and Deirdre O'Connell, Luke Kelly's wife]: Her description of her [Deirdre McCartan] was that she was totally in love with Ronnie. Sabina mentioned, for example, the other Deirdre, Deirdre O'Connell, who was the founder of the Focus Theatre, and she said that when Luke would be travelling abroad the idea that Deirdre O'Connell wouldn't do anything would be regarded as absurd because she would be getting on with her things. But Deirdre McCartan would in fact live for Ronnie coming back. Like in the poem she would pine away for endless periods of time and then there would be an electrifying period of energy when Ronnie was due back.

Tonight with Vincent Browne, RTÉ Radio 1, June 2007

Maybe before there were children and when she was very young – she might have felt a bit lonely when they were off touring England and that. And they did go on these massive tours in the early days – they'd spend eight weeks or so touring England. They spent a lot of time together initially. But then when my sister came along, that would have changed things. I never felt when we were growing up that there was a sense of pining. I think there was the natural sort of missing someone when they're away. If anything, my dad over the years found

it harder to be away and I remember phone calls that they would have and it was my mother reassuring my father rather than the other way around.

Phelim, October 2008

Germany, early 1970s. Ronnie, Barney, Luke, Ciarán and Deirdre with fans

Paddy Drew at a family occasion in the early 1970s; and later, in his workplace, in the 1980s

My grandfather was very, very easygoing. My dad said he'd come back from a tour and he'd go and visit Papa. He used to drink in the Noggin Inn and when Dad would come back from a tour he'd go to see Papa down there, and at that stage Dad was becoming very well known, at least in Dublin. And he'd go down and drop a few quid and he'd say to Papa, 'How'ya, Dad, will you have a pint?' 'Yeah, I'll have a pint and a small one.' And my dad would say, 'Mr O'Byrne, what will you have?' And he'd say, 'Ah thanks, Ronnie, I'll have the same.' 'And Mr Kelly?' 'Yeah.' And then Papa would say, 'And Mr O'Reilly over there in the corner.' And eventually Dad would be buying drinks for the whole pub. That'd be Papa.

Phelim, October 2008

Basically, and for want of a better word, I got homesick on all those three-month tours. Some people are compulsive travellers, but anywhere outside Ireland I'm like a fish out of water . . . I found that the constraints imposed on me as a member of the group were making me stale. It's much easier to experiment and sing new songs as a solo

In the early 1970s Ronnie did a number of fund-raising shows for the Bishop of Kerry, Eamonn Casey. He is seen here in Kerry with Bishop Casey, Fr Michael Cleary, Gay Byrne, and his friend jarvey Nedeen Kelliher.

In 1974 Ciarán Bourke had a brain haemorrhage. Ronnie decided to leave The Dubliners. 'Ronnie had always detested the actual mechanics of the high-speed world of travel they'd had to undertake. Rightly or wrongly he blamed the tours and the travel for Ciarán's now very precarious state of health.' – Mary Hardy, The Dubliners Scrapbook: An Intimate Journal

Ronnie and Deirdre in her mother's house. Early 1970s

performer . . . Also, my inability to keep receipts of expenses on those tours meant that the taxman always got more than his fair share of the proceeds; I'm afraid I have absolutely no business acumen.

Irish Independent, October 1974

The best time in The Dubliners, as far as I'm concerned, was the first eight years. It was all new then. I think what got to Luke was that the group had stagnated and we were just repeating ourselves. Just going through the motions. That's why I left for the first time in 1974.

Irish Examiner, March 2005

In October 1974 Ronnie starred with Niall Toibin in The Bells of Hell, *a show devised by Niall Toibin from the writings of Brendan Behan and from personal recollections, with songs chosen by Ronnie. It was put together in six days as a replacement for a show that had dropped out of that year's Dublin Theatre festival.*

Nine out of ten times Behan put it just as I would have, if I had been there on the spot.

Evening Press, November 1978

There is so much hypocrisy in Dublin. The literary pubs are filled with bores, and the art pubs are filled with frauds. No wonder it's getting hard to get a peaceful drink in Dublin.

Irish Independent, October 1974

Phelim: He enjoys his celebrity, but gives short shrift to begrudgers and those who make unreasonable demands. The morning after a night spent back on the drink, for example, he walked into a pub on his way into town and called for a gin and tonic. The pub was empty except for a man at the far end. My father stood at the bar, drinking his drink, until the silence was broken by the other man. 'I thought you were off the drink,' he said. 'I am,' answered my dad, 'but I have a gin and tonic every now and again. I find it helps me to mind my own business; would you like one?'

Sunday Times, May 2008

Before I worked with him on *The Bells of Hell*, I was a great fan of Toibin's for years. I learned a lot from him, because I was open to it. Toibin taught me a lot about storytelling and he's someone I'm very fond of. I love his humour. I love how every time you ring him up

it's always, 'Hmmm, what do you want?' I find that very funny. In my business you have a circle of friends, but it's an abstract. You don't see them all the time: you're not in the same place every weekend. Often you go ages without seeing each other, but the friendship survives. It might be months or years, but everyone understands how it works.

Sunday Independent, February 2005

I always hate the word 'curmudgeon' being used in the wrong sense – a bitter and twisted old fart. Whereas people like my dad and Niall they're not bitter against other people's success, but they'd be true curmudgeons in terms of an absolute neurotic fixation with things that don't work. And because they're intelligent men they just cannot understand how somebody could promote something that could work badly or the promotion of the mediocre.

Phelim, October 2008

I don't like meetings and besides I am too intolerant and would probably be kicked out. Any meetings I have gone to in the past, however well intentioned or well behaved I am, it just doesn't work out.

Evening Press, November 1978

With Dad there was always a sort of double-edged sword, where he liked to sort of keep you on your toes. Sometimes I wished he could have just lightened up a bit and not taken life so seriously all the time. I understand what he was going through; in his situation, life was always ever only going to be what he made it. There wasn't a point where he could say, 'Ah, I think I'll take it easy.' That came later on.

I'm an actor and I also can be quite shy and I think my dad had that shyness about him as well but he coped with that by being almost defensive. He was ready for people all the time – which is exhausting. And by God, they're out there, but not all the time. Sometimes people would approach him and if he wasn't in good humour he could give them short shrift and sometimes you'd be, 'Aw, Dad, they're only just coming up to say "hi".' Like the people that he would meet could be a bit inarticulate because maybe they'd be in awe, but he couldn't actually understand that. It wasn't in his realm of experience that you could be that in awe of somebody.

Phelim, October 2008

Phelim: One morning when I was a child, I approached my father while he was reading a newspaper. 'Dad,' I said. 'Yes,' he replied, without lowering the paper. 'You know the moon?' 'Yes.' 'And you know the sun?' 'Yes.' 'Well, where does the moon go when the sun comes up and where does the sun go when the moon comes up?' Quietly and without ambiguity, he said, 'Phelim, don't ever ask me a question like that again; I don't know and I don't care.' To which I responded, 'Well, Declan's dad –' 'Well,' he cut in, 'go down and ask Declan's dad.' My father has always been clear about what interests him, and equally clear about what does not.

Sunday Times, May 2008

That period he was freelance in the seventies was very difficult; there was very little interest in live music. I remember travelling around with Dad when I was about fourteen or so, it would have been about 1983, when he did solo gigs, and they were depressing affairs. Going down to some small town on a cold January Wednesday night and the people there just not interested in listening; all they were there for was the jar. And that's why I think when he did the one-man show

One of his many gigs during his freelance years in the late 1970s was taking part in the historical series Irishmen and Irishwomen *on RTÉ. Ronnie told the story of Justin McCarthy, commander of the Irish Brigade in France. 'We always watched him, whatever he was doing. We never took it for granted when he was on television doing anything.' – Cliodhna*

that he was very intent on playing small theatres and arts centres. The days of playing pubs were over.

I remember one particular occasion. I had learned from Benny Lynch, who was the sound operator for The Dubliners, how to operate this little four-channel sound desk. I travelled down with Dad and my Uncle Tony and a guitar player called Bobby Kelly who was accompanying Dad at the time and Dad had this gig down the country and I'll never forget it. It was just after the seventies and there was no development in the town: I'd say it'd been the same way since 1942. It was just a grey, colourless kind of place. I remember we were staying over the pub on the corner of the square. We didn't have time to drop the bags by the time we got down there, so we just went straight down to the venue.

The place was stuffed but it was one of those rowdy gigs – people weren't listening, Dad was just going, 'Play the gig, get it over with,

Paddy and Maureen O'Donoghue
15 Merrion Row, Dublin 2
Telephone 62807

Mr. RONNIE DREW.
BENEVENAGH
GREYSTONES
CO. WICKLOW

DEAR RONNIE,
WE ARE RETIRING FROM BUSINESS
ON THE 7TH OCTOBER, A DATE WE WOULD LIKE
TO KEEP TO OURSELVES OTHERWISE THE
SOUVENEER HUNTERS WILL CLAIM ALL OUR
PRECIOUS MEMORIES FROM THE BACK ROOM.
WE TAKE THIS OPPORTUNITY OF
THANKING YOU. OUR AMBASSADOR FOR CONTRIBUT-
-ING TO MAKING O'D THE INSTITUTION IT
BECAME.
WE FEEL SAD AT HAVING TO
RETIRE BUT OUR HEALTH POSITION DOES NOT
ALLOW US TO CONTINUE FOR MUCH LONGER IN
BUSINESS AND LIKE YOURSELVE WE ARE NOT
GETTING ANY YOUNGER.
WE ARE GOING TO `LIVE IN YOUR
HOME GROUND AND WE WILL CONTACT YOU
WHEN WE ARE SETTLED IN OUR NEW HOME.
YOU WILL ALWAYS HAVE A SPECIAL
PLACE IN OUR HEARTS.
WISHING YOU + DEIRDRE + CHILDREN
EVERY HAPPINESS + SUCCESS
GOD BLESS YOU
LOVE
PADDY + MAUREEN.

Maureen and Paddy O'Donoghue's letter to Ronnie when they retired in the late seventies get off, get paid, go home.' He hadn't been finished about ten minutes when I was clearing up the cables and there was this big stout guy, wearing an open-necked seventies shirt, sitting on a seat singing Meatloaf songs and all these people standing around him and I swear to God they gave him more attention than they gave me dad, but in actual fact they were working themselves up towards the disco. That was the whole point of the evening.

We went back to the hotel and Dad was having a few jars at the time and he went into the bar and this was the only light at the end of the tunnel of the day, the few jars afterwards. And Tony and Bobby and Dad were standing in the bar with the owner of the hotel and they were telling stories and having a bit of crack. Of course, I was only fourteen or so, and I stood there for a while and then I got a pain in me face so I decided to go to bed. And when I went up to bed I walked into the room and it was like walking into the cold room in a butcher's. I opened the door and it was just freezing and I think the window was slightly open and broken so it couldn't close properly so it was damp. I remember peeling back the covers and the sheets were actually wet, they were so damp.

So I went back down to Dad and I tried to interrupt him and he was a bit sort of, 'Yeah, yeah, what do you want?' So I said, 'Could you ask' – I was trying to appear not to be a wimp in front of everybody else – 'could you ask the man does he have any hot-water bottles?' So Dad says, 'For fuck's sake, would you go on outta dat, with your hot-water bottles. Go up to bed and I'll be up in a minute.' So I went up and I got into bed fully clothed, overcoat and everything. And I got in and I found a position that, if I didn't move, was relatively comfortable.

About twenty minutes later Dad came in. He had a routine. I was well used to sharing a room with him travelling around the place. He'd come in, get undressed down to his underpants and then he'd go into the bathroom and he'd have a little read of his book in the bathroom and then he'd come in and he'd get into bed and he'd go to sleep. That was his routine. But he came in and I'll never forget just hearing this, 'O, sweet heart of Jesus!' I could hear him gradually taking his clothes off and, kind of heart-stopping, like, 'Oh, my God!' He was such a creature of habit he tiptoed into the bathroom and once he hit the tiles it was like, 'Oh my Jaysus!' The routine in the *bathroom was cut short because it was obviously far too cold to concentrate on reading a book or anything like that, so he came back in and he got into bed. And I was waiting for it. As soon as his skin hit the sheet he just let this roar out of him. 'Jesus Christ!' And I just said, 'I told you it was cold.' 'You didn't tell me it was this fuckin' cold.' He was giving out because I hadn't protested loudly enough when I went down looking for hot-water bottles.*

And I remember him telling me once he went to bed in a hotel down in Kenmare or somewhere like that and similarly there was a window that was broken and wouldn't shut and he went to bed with his overcoat on and he had a sheepskin overcoat, so it was grand and he was probably a bit pissed anyway. But he woke up and there was snow in the room with him.

Phelim, October 2008

When Ronnie left The Dubliners, Jim McCann took over for him and he left the group again when Ronnie returned in January 1979. This picture of the group on O'Connell Street includes both men and shows them with the tools of their former trades: Ciarán Bourke, the agriculture student, with a crook ('Ciarán was very sick there – he would have been using that crook.' – Phelim); Jim McCann in a white coat (a former medical student); Barney McKenna with mallet (for working as a navvy); John Sheahan with wires (he was a former ESB worker); Luke Kelly as a dishwasher; and Ronnie as a telephone operator.

Shortly before he was due to rejoin the group, Ronnie had a car accident in Portlaoise and broke his hip.

When he was discharged from hospital, there were periods of depression when Ronnie felt he would never get back to full mobility. He would then phone the stables where his horses were kept and instruct them tersely to 'sell the horses'. Deirdre Drew, Ronnie's wife, would then either take herself off to the stables or else phone and say, 'Ignore him!' The stables staff and the trainer were doubtless very confused, but Deirdre knew that the day would dawn when Ronnie would once again be fit to take to the saddle. That day was brought nearer over the Christmas period, when Ronnie was given a completely new hip in a Dublin hospital. After the surgery he used first a walking frame, then two sticks. By the time 1981 dawned, he was getting around with just one stick and looking forward to the day when that too could be put away.

Mary Hardy, UK tour programme notes, 1981

He had a steel hip because he was too young to have a plastic one. There were three or four years where he had the steel hip in, and he always had to have a stick with that. And then, when he had the plastic hip put in, he didn't. And that plastic hip was heading for,

'That's our one and only package holiday. That's in Mijas in Spain. You can see the stick there. I was thirteen. It wasn't anything we ever did. It must have been after the crash and maybe just Dad needed a holiday.' – Cliodhna. The man in the bottom picture is Joe Hackett, Ronnie's old friend from his days as a language teacher in Seville.

certainly, twenty-five years. If he got very tired, or jarred, he would limp, but other than that he was fine.

Cliodhna, October 2008

He found it very difficult to switch off. It was sometimes difficult because there'd be times when I used to say, 'Jesus, could we not just all sit around and not say anything?' Dad always demanded your attention. He was in his head a lot. Even if you agreed with what he was saying, he would still argue with you because he had thought so much about his point that he had to vent this opinion. And it would very often be that you'd be sitting around having dinner and you wouldn't be talking about George Bush and the Bush administration but he would just suddenly start talking about it. You might say, 'Jesus, that's a great job they've done on the road out there.' 'And another thing about . . .' He would just completely dismiss what you were talking about and launch into this lecture. But then obviously he was in his element when he was out at a dinner party and he'd get a chance to have a good argument with somebody about something to do with bureaucracy or social injustice.

Phelim, October 2008

Ronnie made his return to The Dubliners at a concert at Caesar's Palace in Luton in January 1979. He was still unable to stand.

Con Houlihan: There is one number in the show that in itself made the night unforgettable. It is that greatest of all anti-war songs, 'And the Band Played Waltzing Matilda'. Ronnie sang it – and in all the years I have known him he has never moved me so deeply. And quite clearly the big audience felt that way too – the effect was profound and the applause was long and loud and from the heart. And that number was a shattering reminder that there is far more to The Dubliners than lively music and ribald songs. What makes them so great is that their talents are infused with fine intelligence and wry integrity.

Evening Press, July 1979

Ronnie, Old Gravel Voice himself, walked out on a crutch, a reminder of his recent car accident, but once he sat on his stool and opened his

Ronnie in costume for his role as Jacob in Joseph and the Amazing Technicolor Dreamcoat *in autumn 1983*

mouth, it was the Drew of old. It is still hard to imagine The Dubliners without Ronnie, even though he was away from them for nearly five years.

Evening Herald, July 1979

Ronnie and Seán Cannon on tour

In 1980 Luke Kelly had a brain tumour removed. Eamonn Campbell joined the group to cover for his absence. Galway-born Seán Cannon formally joined The Dubliners in autumn 1982. In 1983 Noel Pearson's long stretch as the group's manager came to an amicable end, and John Sheahan took over as manager. And in January 1984 Luke had a seizure before going on stage in Mannheim and was taken to hospital in Heidelberg before being sent home. He died in Dublin on 30 January.

[on visiting Luke in hospital in Heidelberg shortly after his collapse in Mannheim]: We sat there chatting, I suppose, for about three or four hours. But there wasn't any angst or it wasn't angst-ridden. Or it wasn't 'no regrets' or 'my old friend' – no sentimentality; we just chatted. But we *really* chatted. And I'm always delighted we had that

long conversation with Luke shortly before he died because after that
we continued on with the tour in Germany. Luke came home and
went back to the doctor here and he went into hospital here and he
died on 30 January. I was there when he died. It was tragic really,
because he was only forty-four and I think he had an awful lot more
in him that hadn't come out by that time.

Interview with Colm Keane, *Seven Drunken Nights*, RTÉ Radio 1,
March 2002

Ronnie's favourite Luke Kelly story is when a fully paid-up drunk in
a pub once said to him, 'If I had a gun, I'd join the IRA.' To which
Luke replied, 'If you had a gun, you'd pawn it.'

46A magazine, May 1998

*The time Luke died sticks in my mind because Papa died that year as
well, 1984. I have a very vivid memory of going up to him and he
was putting his cufflinks on in the bedroom and he was really, really
upset. It was like losing a brother. People sort of slag off actors about
being luvvies and you're always hugging each other and all that. The
thing about it is when you've worked so intensively with people over
a short period you do form a bond – even if you don't see each other
from one end of the year to the next, or even for five years, when you*

A publicity shot of the group in 1983, with Luke wearing a cap to cover the signs of his surgery

do meet there's a real feeling of celebration because you've got so much in common and you know so much about each other. That's just an actor doing a run. They would have spent so much time on the road together and waiting for hours in airports and travelling on buses for hours and playing Scrabble together and falling out and falling back in again.

Phelim, October 2008

I think I was probably a bit jealous of him, you know, but it didn't last very long. He was very generous. It took a little while to get to know him. There was no rivalry. I was close to him, but he'd be shouting, you know, 'Fuck off' and all that. Luke was the communist, but I didn't quite agree – for instance, I used to ask him why, if communism was so great, so many people wanted to get out of communist countries? He used to get very annoyed.

Village, December 2006

Luke liked to talk about left-wing politics. I suppose he was a bit of a rebel socialist in the sense that he couldn't abide the party line. Sometimes I remember days would go by on tour and we wouldn't talk to each other. Then Luke would start talking and our conversation would go on for a long time. At times he could be introspective, even a loner. If anything was bothering him, I think he found it hard to confide in someone in the group . . . He couldn't tolerate sham or conceit, for instance. He enjoyed the crack. The Dubliners always loved the crack. I couldn't laugh like him. When he thought something was really funny, he laughed at it. And another thing, he never sang a song for the sake of singing it. He always tried to make it meaningful . . . When Luke died it was a strange brotherly thing. The Dubliners had, it seemed to us, lost a brother.

Entertainer, September 1985

With Luke and myself there was a kind of thread. At first, when I'd hear his voice, I'd get a very eerie feeling, that he was kind of looking over my shoulder. But nowadays, when I hear him suddenly, say if

John Sheahan, Seán Cannon and Ronnie playing at the opening of the Luke Kelly Bridge over the Tolka at Ballybough in 1987

I'm driving along in the car, I get a very vivid picture of the whole thing. He was a great strength in The Dubliners. I found it difficult at first: 'How are we going to fill this void?' But, like everything else, you just have to get on with it and hope for the best.

RTÉ Guide, November 1995

Phil Coulter: I have often tried to analyse the appeal of The Dubliners. It wasn't merely that they were all individually talented; it wasn't just that each was a character in his own right; it wasn't even that they were the first. It was all of those things and more. When those five guys walked on stage something magical happened. They weren't a ballad group, they were a national institution. Twenty years before the music business discovered the phenomenon of 'street credibility' The Dubliners had mastered it. They *were* the first. They blazed a trail through the Aran curtain of singing jumpers just being themselves and damn the begrudgers.

Irish Times, February 1984

Dad was sitting at the bar in this hotel in Germany one morning after a gig. He was having a cup of coffee at the bar. And this young fellow came in with a leather jacket and he said, 'Howya, Ronnie.' He was a real young fellow and Dad said, 'Hello, son, howya.'

And he said, 'How're you gettin' on?'

Dad says, 'I'm grand.'

'You doing a few gigs here?'

'Yeah, yeah. We were in the concert hall,' or whatever it was.

'Oh, very good. Yeah.'

Me dad said, 'Would you like a drink or something?'

He said, 'Ah, I'll have a cup of coffee.'

So Dad ordered him a cup of coffee and sat down. Me dad thought, 'This young fellow is probably working on a building site, poor fellow. He probably misses home and he's delighted to see me.' And he felt sorry for him.

'So how are things? Are you over here doing a bit of work yourself?'

He goes: 'Yeah, yeah. Just here for a couple of nights.'

'Ah right, yeah. And what are you doing?'

'We're playing in the arena outside town.'

And Dad's thinking, 'Oh Jaysus. We're playing in this hall to about four or five thousand people but the arena holds about 25,000 people.' He thought, 'Jesus Christ, this young fellow's obviously in a band.'

So he goes, 'Oh, you're playing out the road. Very good. Well done. That sounds great. And what band are you playing with? Oh, U2. Very good.'

And that was Dad's story of how he met Larry Mullen for the first time.

Phelim, October 2008

Edge, U2: I ran into Ronnie in a hotel bar in Germany after a gig. Bang, straight into Ronnie. I was kind of stunned because it's kind of like meeting the pope, or Eamon de Valera or somebody. You're not expecting it. And he came out with the best line, which I've remembered ever since. He said, 'Edge, I would take it as a great honour if I could tell my children that you bought me a drink.'

The Late Late Show, RTÉ One, February 2008

BP Fallon [on a conversation with Ronnie in Cannes in the mid-1980s]: Mr Drew was not a happy man. Fed up with The Dubliners. Fed up with making the continual concessions to other people's foibles that are often forced upon you when you play in a band. Fed up with what he felt was repetition and being stuck in a rut. Just fed up. 'I've had enough,' Ronnie said. 'I'm going to leave the band.' He leant back in his deckchair and perused the heavens. 'Don't tell anyone – I haven't told the lads yet.' Well, he'd left in 1974, after twelve years behind the mast. Rejoined in 1979 and, this being the mid-eighties, had a wee bit to go yet before he departed again in 1996.

The Best of Ronnie Drew, sleeve notes, 2007

Mam had her own thing as well – she went through a sort of mid-life crisis in the eighties. I think she was just feeling a little bit like, 'What have I achieved?' I think she might have harboured aspirations to maybe run an antique shop or something like that, which never really came to fruition. I don't think she felt incomplete as a mother or as a wife but just professionally I think she felt that maybe she could have done more with her talents. She wanted to take some time off from

Cliodhna's twenty-first birthday, 1986

being a mother and a wife, and she took off to America for what was to be three months or four months with two friends of hers. And Dad just couldn't hack it without her so she had to come back a little bit early. But I think she'd kind of got that out of her system a bit. Her way of dealing with things was she'd just go quite quiet. You didn't discuss personal feelings. And yet I could ring my mother and if I was really in difficulty, say, in a relationship, or if I was just feeling low about stuff, I could talk to her and she was great. If I was to sit down and tell my problems to my father, he would listen intently, but then he would just say, 'Ah, don't worry, it'll be grand.' It was almost like he wasn't able to process or deal with that kind of stuff.

Phelim, October 2008

Ronnie and Deirdre's twenty-fifth wedding anniversary dinner

I've never met anybody who lived in the present as much as they did. My mother never really harped on about the past or the future. It was always just about now. It was almost an innate quality that she had. I used to love sitting with my mother if she had friends in, and they'd be sitting there chatting and smoking and drinking tea and nothing in the world existed except this. And there was just a lovely sort of

*Deirdre in typical pose, at the kitchen table, with Seán Óg McKenna,
Barney's brother*

*Deirdre with film producer Kevin McClory and singer-songwriter Donal
McDonald in the mid-1990s*

warmth, and 'Miriam has these curtains,' and 'Jesus, did you hear about such-a-thing?' My mother wouldn't be gossiping. No malice in it. Just chat. And I used to sit there soaking it up. I used to love the feeling of the warmth and the cosiness of the chat and 'Come on, we'll open another packet of fags.' There was a great sort of devil-may-care attitude and it was not hurting anybody.

Phelim, October 2008

[on recording 'The Irish Rover' with The Pogues]: We first met [The Pogues] in Vienna, at a folk festival. They had mentioned that they'd noticed us. Here was a group of young fellows giving the kind of thing we'd been doing a different treatment. In the same way as we had been giving it a different treatment when we started. What they were saying to me is that they were more or less singing an emigrant's memory of what Irish music is like. To me that's quite valid. I never had to sing as fast in my life as with Shane MacGowan on this record. But I managed it. It's exciting. It's a new thing for us to do. They're all grand lads.

Hot Press, December 1986

We'd met The Pogues but we didn't really know them, but I think their lack of self-importance appealed to us. They didn't take themselves too seriously.

Sunday Independent, February 2005

I really enjoyed that collaboration with The Pogues. I really did. Again, it's not a great deep song or anything, but I really enjoyed it. I got a fantastic uplift from the whole thing. It was just a great feeling: get up there and have drums and all goin' and you're singing. It was just a good feeling. I think certain songs are there just to be enjoyed, not to be dissected and what does this mean and what does that mean. There are other songs that merit that kind of treatment, but that one is there for pure enjoyment.

Interview with Colm Keane, *Seven Drunken Nights*, RTÉ Radio 1,
March 2002

Price £1.50 incl taxes (£1.40 Northern Ireland only)

Free Pull-Out Music Calendar Inside

HOT PRESS

Ho Ho Ho & a Bottle of Rum!
Christmas with Ronnie Drew & Shane McGowan

The Derry City Story
by Eamonn McCann

READERS' POLL
Vote Now!

1986 REVISITED

+

The London-Irish • FRANK CLUSKEY • The Condom King
XTC • Something Happens! • ALICE COOPER
Quiz Of The Century • FUN! FUN! FUN!

80 PAGE BUMPER NEW YEAR SPECIAL

The Right Honourable the Lord Mayor of Dublin, Alderman Bertie Ahern, T.D.

cordially invites

Ronnie & Deirdre Drew

TO A CIVIC RECEPTION

TO HONOUR THE DUBLINERS

on the occasion of their 25th year in Show Business

in the Oak Room. Mansion House. Dawson Street, Dublin 2

on Thursday 7th May, 1987 at 8.00 p.m.

R.S.V.P.
Mansion House,
Dublin 2. Tel. 761845

Please present this Card

[on the success of The Dubliners after twenty-five years]: I think that there could be something in the fact that nobody ever tried to change us. People like Noel Pearson, who used to manage us, or Jim Hand, our present manager, they let us do our own thing, let us be ourselves. That could have something to do with it.

RTÉ Guide, April 1987

I really found it gratifying when Bono and the lads turned up on our twenty-fifth anniversary show and spoke of how they respect us and realize what we've done for groups like U2 as well as for traditional musicians. I just wish more groups like them would look back into their roots.

Irish Times, July 1992

Dad got a second wind from working with The Pogues and The Late Late *and everything. He loved it. It was great crack. There was great excitement in our house. Dad had left The Dubliners once or twice, because there was a sort of sense of covering old ground again. But then when this happened it really breathed new life into things. And it was also the idea that this young band, which was hugely successful,*

The Dubliners in 1987 on The Late Late Show *celebration show: Ronnie, Barney and John from the early days with more recent additions, Eamonn Campbell and Seán Cannon*

Ronnie with Christy Moore and Bono, Edge and Larry from U2, the night of The Late Late Show Dubliners *special*

BRITISH CONSULATE GENERAL
55 PUBLIC SQUARE, SUITE 1650
CLEVELAND OHIO 44113-1963
TEL: 216 621-7674
TELEX 980-126 (AB BRITIAN Clv)
FAX (216) 621-2615

The Dubliners
c/o Vista International   11 March 1988
Pittsburgh, PA

Dear Dubliners.

I am commanded by HRH The Prince of Wales to thank you for
your good wishes on the occasion of his visit to
Pittsburgh.

It was a pity that His Royal Highness missed you. I,
however, am a frequent visitor to the Vista, and will look
out for you with a view to drinking his guinness.

Good wishes,

Yours sincerely,

John Sharland

E J SHARLAND
H M Consul General

EJS:he

'The Prince of Wales was in the same hotel as The Dubliners and Dad
sent some message to him. They couldn't believe they got a message back.'
— Phelim

considered them this huge influence, and getting the attention from younger bands.

Phelim, October 2008

Gay Byrne: Two weeks after the show I received a picture postcard from some foreign clime. It was signed by The Dubliners. And it said simply, 'Thanks, head, for the remould.'

The Dubliners: 30 Years A-Greying Tour, UK programme notes, 1992

BP Fallon: There's an air of easygoingness about The Dubliners, a refreshing lack of franticness, of *flash*. After their recent *Late Late* outing, while everyone else milled around in the hospitality room, Ronnie Drew was happy to stand at the door and chat away to the security man. *Normal* carry-on.

Sunday Tribune, March 1987

I always regarded him as a member, even when he wasn't playing with us any more. He was always translating pieces for us and was still on the lookout for material. It's more like losing a brother, because he really was part of a family.

Irish Times, May 1988

Dad was always encouraging us to do classes and he was always delighted when I was doing the guitar but he didn't really get involved – just let us at it. Dad was always very encouraging, very supportive. He always enjoyed the stage and was very happy for my involvement in the theatre. I used to play music locally, small-time stuff, more of a hobby than anything else, and occasionally he would get up with us, but in general he didn't get involved. He more or less left it up to you to do your own thing. I suppose I'd have liked it if he'd got involved a bit more, given some sort of instruction, but that was just my parents' way.

Phelim, October 2008

BP Fallon: Sometimes Ronnie Drew lets his insecurities run rampant and he's doing it now. You tell him yet again that people *love* him, that other superb artists like Christy Moore and Elvis Costello admire

Ronnie sings to his mother, Peg,
at her eightieth birthday party in 1988.

The Drew family celebrating their mother's eightieth birthday in 1988:
Tony, Margie, Joan, Peg, Gerry and Ronnie

Ciarán Bourke died in May 1988. He had been left semi-paralysed by a brain haemorrhage in 1974. His last appearance with the group was on The Late Late Show *tribute, when he recited 'The Lament for Brendan Behan' by Joe Ó Broin. He is shown here in the studio that night.*

him enormously. 'Do they,' he says, his eyes sad through his glasses. 'Do they really?' . . . He tells a story about how when he was in Spain years ago as a younger man, he saw a prisoner being taken off a train. The unfortunate captive was handcuffed between two policemen, yet

Phelim and friend Tom Galvin, gigging in a local pub, late 1980s

'Mam couldn't sing. She never tried. She had a good ear and she knew what was good and what wasn't, but she never sang. I'd only play if there was nobody in the room. I would like to be able to play but would want to do it brilliantly and maybe I never took the time to make myself brilliant.' – Cliodhna

managed to fumble in his clothes to find the butt of a cigarette. One of the guards made a play of lighting it, then cruelly [knocked] it to the ground. 'I don't care if he was a murderer,' Ronnie reflects. 'That was no way to treat a fellow human being.' The incident stuck in Ronnie's mind and he recites the lines he wrote about this event: 'Great oak trees/crushing a thorny stick/and always crushing/for one tiny prick.'

Sunday Tribune, October 1988

Jim McCann, Eamonn Campbell, Paddy Moloney of The Chieftains, and Ronnie picking up their shovels for a tree-planting initiative, Ballymun, 1988

I like Ronnie Drew on television. His ordinariness is extraordinary because it is real and is to be treasured in a folk music milieu where barflies and slummers abound, affecting unnaturally 'natural' personas and where 'salt of the earth' is too often equated with deliberately mispronouncing Dublin as 'Dubbelin'.

Review of the TV documentary *The Dubliners' Dublin*, *Irish Independent*, November 1988

Billy Connolly: He stopped a fight between me and Dominic Behan. I was waiting to see them after the concert, which I had loved. And

Ronnie taking tea with Billy Connolly when Connolly was touring Ireland

Dominic was there. I'd never met him before. I wasn't sure who he was. He said something and I took umbrage. We were growling and actually came to blows and Ronnie jumped in the middle of it. That was the night of the long knives when I met Ronnie Drew and we were joined at the hip after that.

September Song, RTÉ One, May 2008

Con Houlihan: The Dubliners were less a group than a meitheal. In the old peasant pattern the meitheal came together to do a job – and that was it. The Dubliners were all individualists – Luke and Ronnie and Ciarán and John and Barney were leaves from different trees blown together by the wind that changed the world of music a generation ago. What they had in common was artistic honesty.

The Dubliners: 30 Years A-Greying Tour, UK programme notes, 1992

John Sheahan is the only member of the group to have a formal musical education. He was rather proud of this status until quite recently when an old man in a rural district of Ireland came up to him

*On Greystones Beach after Cliodhna's wedding
to David Dunne in May 1991*

Ronnie and Phelim singing at Cliodhna's wedding. Phelim's hair was shorn because he was appearing in The Plough and the Stars *at the Abbey.*

Ronnie with his first grandchild, Ruaidhrí Dunne, in 1995, when he was nearly three. Though he retained his love of horses, Ronnie never got back into riding the way he had before hurting his hip.

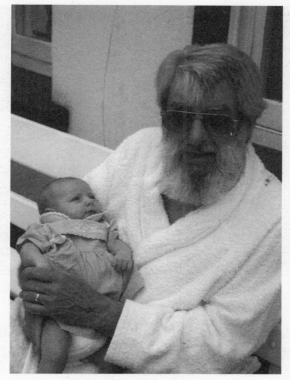

With Aoife, Ruaidhrí's sister, in 1995

following a concert and said, 'Tell me, young fellow, do you read music or are you gifted?'

The Dubliners: 30 Years A-Greying Tour, UK programme notes, 1992

Barney's telling us how technically he's the longest serving member of the band – the original founder member, Ronnie Drew, having taken a couple of years sabbatical in the seventies. John Sheahan growls at him, 'You're the longest serving and I'm the longest *suffering*.'

Folk Roots, March 1993

Fans are more strict about being into classical or jazz or whatever, but musicians embrace all disciplines. Take someone like Louis Stewart, one of the top jazz guitarists in the world. I couldn't keep myself warm on guitar beside Louis, but I'm godfather to his son,

Ronnie and Louis Stewart

Anthony. In this business, you just fall in with people, and you meet them under the strangest circumstances.

Sunday Independent, February 2005

Rory [Gallagher] and I struck up a nice friendship, without living in each other's pockets. He wanted to hear tapes I had of Seosamh Ó hEanaigh and Maggie Barry and all, and I used to send them to him. Then he wrote a song for me, 'Barley and Grape Rag', and I sang it with him at a public concert outside the bank on College Green. That was one of my favourite moments, ever, because I respected him so much.

I was embarrassed, I suppose, at Rory's funeral, when one of his brothers asked me to help carry the coffin. I felt a bit out of things, because there were a lot of blues guys there, but then I thought to hell with what other people think. I didn't want anyone to think I was pushing myself forward, but it would have been churlish to say not. I'm glad now to say I carried his coffin, because I have great memories of him.

Sunday Independent, February 2005

Ronnie at the Rory Gallagher blues masterclass in the Guinness Hop Store in August 1992

Seosamh Ó hEanaigh, who was a great *sean nós* singer, he was very fond of us. Ciarán MacMathúna takes us seriously. But we're not polished enough to be accepted by the business community – they think we're slightly trampish. And they haven't been told by any authority which they respect – although I don't know what authority that is – that we're good, bad or indifferent. So they don't quite know whether to like us or not. I went to a concert of Louis's [Louis Stewart] in the Concert Hall and there was all these jazz buffs there . . . all these fellas looking at me: 'What's *he* doing at *our* concert?'

Sunday Tribune, August 1988

Dad had a fascination with the British upper class. He loved the way that the British upper class did things. How when you meet aristocracy – not faux aristocracy but the real thing – they're generally really nice people and have no illusions about life and they're generally very good fun and take it for granted that things would be fresh and that things would be of the highest quality in terms of clothes and in terms of cars. Just this disdain for the mediocre. I think he just loved that fresh take on life: 'Oh come on, let's go and have lunch and to hell with it all.'

The actor Jack McGowran was a great friend of Dad's and after his death his wife, Gloria, stayed friends with Mam and Dad and I spent time with her in London when I was over there. Gloria is terribly grand. She introduced him to Simpsons in the Strand. It's a real old-school place and Dad loved it because it was all that public schoolboy stuff, up in London, go to this place, a big side of beef on trolleys, a huge feed. And he loved Hunter's in Ashford for that. Because it had that old-world gentility about it. While he was under no illusion that he could become part of that world, I think he always felt if you have a few bob, why not enjoy it.

Phelim, October 2008

In September 1994 the Drews threw a massive party to celebrate Ronnie's sixtieth birthday. Nearly 400 dinners were served that night and they had a tent and Portaloos in the back garden.

Ronnie with Deirdre, Cliodhna and his mother, Peg. Phelim was in the Ukraine filming an episode of the Sharpe television series, Sharpe's Battle. 'I remember ringing that morning and it was awful. I really wanted to be there.'

Christy Moore leading the singing. Left of Christy, Patsy Watchorn; behind Christy, John Sheahan; and right, Jimmy Crowley. 'It was a freezing night, that's why Christy was in the garden in his cap.' – Cliodhna

The crush of people in the hallway includes: Simon Carmody and Fiachna Ó Braonáin (under the doorframe), Seán Cannon (under the far painting) and a partial view of Harriet Roche, secretary to The Dubliners (in the lower-left-hand corner). 'Ciarán lived in Sandymount after his brain haemorrhage and he hated the meals-on-wheels food and Harriet used to work for AIB Bank Centre and they had decent food in there so she used to bring him down some. She kind of became his angel: she really minded him.' – Cliodhna

Ronnie and Barney

'Mam's only like that because of the camera. She hated having her photo taken. Hated it. She wasn't at all stern.' – Cliodhna

On the road in Germany with Eamonn Campbell in the early nineties. 'The only time I ever saw him in shorts was going swimming.' – Phelim

When Dad was seventy in 2004 Mam was sick for the first time. She was going to do a party for him but then she was in hospital and she had a tumour and had half a lung removed. But she had had an all-clear though, just before she got sick again in 2007.

Cliodhna, October 2008

In September 1995 Ronnie announced that he was quitting The Dubliners at the end of the year.

Deirdre with Ronnie backstage after his last concert as a member of The Dubliners in Hamburg on 9 December 1995

Shane MacGowan: The Dubliners were the band that made me realize that good Irish music was basically the same as rock 'n' roll or any good music – it hits you in the heart, soul, groin and feet . . .

From The Dubliners' album *Milestones*, sleeve notes, 1995

The adventure of the journey

John Sheahan

I first saw Ronnie in the early sixties when he was performing with John Molloy at the Gate Theatre. As well as acting in sketches with John, he appeared in front of the curtain at the interval, singing long ballads such as 'Van Diemen's Land' and 'Skibbereen'. His voice was startling; I had never heard anything like it before. His presence was riveting and, against all odds, he cast a spell on an audience that was anything but captive.

Charisma and presence are qualities impossible to define, but Ronnie had them in full measure. He was a gifted entertainer and storyteller – his natural environment, the pub – surrounded by a large circle of friends, all leaning in to catch every nuance of the yarn. His timing and turn of phrase held your undivided attention, but if your concentration wavered, he sensed it and devoured you without apology.

He hated his flow to be interrupted, and if a barman arrived with an order in the middle of a story, Ronnie's gestures and body language made it clear that he should keep a safe distance until the punchline was delivered. He was a master at painting a picture with words, and he saw the delivery of a song as a natural extension of the storyteller's art. A song had to have a good storyline or it wasn't worth singing. Within the context of The Dubliners this celebration of life in the pub enjoyed a smooth transition to the concert hall.

He had an impish sense of humour. In the early days, when I still had my day job with the ESB, I was anxious to get on the road for home after country gigs, but of course there was always the inevitable 'one for the road'. On one occasion, after a gig in Tipperary, I attempted to close the bar after several 'last' rounds by surreptitiously tipping the young barman a fiver. However, my plan failed and on the way home I told Ronnie what had happened. 'Ah!' says Ronnie, 'I saw what you were up to – I gave him a tenner to keep it open!'

Stories about drink were often exaggerated, but this one had its humorous side: We were playing at the Gleneagle Hotel in Killarney – all tuned up and ready to go on stage, but no sign of Ronnie. Was he on the gargle? Would he turn up? We were about to go on without him when an American tourist burst in through the dressing-room door announcing: 'I'm delivering your leader.' It transpired that Ronnie had picked up this hitch-hiker earlier in the day and, realizing that he himself was in no condition for driving, asked the tourist if he could drive on the left-hand side. He assured Ronnie that he could; they swopped places and so started a chauffeured pub crawl around his beloved Kerry for the rest of the day.

He was a transient being who had difficulty with the notion of planning for a future that might never happen. He was superstitious about investing in pension funds in case he was tempting fate. Instead, he lived for the moment, immersing himself in the immediacy of the craic at hand. At the end of a day's journey that involved stops and sessions at rural pubs where we had the craic with local musicians and storytellers, he would be in top form. The journey to the gig was as much an adventure as the gig itself. This was the stuff of life. It was all like a play that might never be run again, so every moment had to be savoured. When asked about life on the road in the early days, he replied, 'We had a party that went on for thirty years.' This summed up his attitude to life.

He was cynical about politicians, believing that the country could be better run by a small group of dedicated businessmen. 'We have a very expensive government to keep,' he would say, in mock defence of tax increases in a budget.

He could sometimes be brusque and impatient, but the gruff exterior was often a cover for shyness. He was sensitive, well read, extremely charitable, and had a strong sense of the spiritual.

My life was enriched when our paths crossed about forty-four years ago. I little realized then that my hobby would become my life when I agreed to fill in during the 'porter break' at a Dubliners' gig in Howth.

The man with the strange voice that startled me in the Gate Theatre back in the early sixties became a life-long friend.

The picture on page 185 shows John Sheahan at the reception after Ronnie's funeral.

No room for ambiguity

Niall Toibin

In the early sixties, Frank Walsh ran a splendid, now forgotten pub in Ranelagh called the Chariot Inn, where some of Ireland's budding entertainers flexed their musical muscles, among them Seámus Ennis, Paddy Moloney and some other Chieftains to be. Breandán Ó Dúill was joined now and again by two of the great voices-to-be of Irish balladry: carrot-haired Luke Kelly and raven-black Ronnie Drew.

At the time I was a contracted member of the Radio Éireann Players, but mitched now and again in the Chariot and inevitably fell in love and in line with the romantic left-wing ideology of the times. I even sang, of which more anon, the less the better.

I must here record an intrusion into the love life of Ronnie and

Deirdre. A close friend of Dr Pat McCartan, Deirdre's father, was having a pint with me in my local. He was a prominent member of Clann na Poblachta, Pat's party. He mentioned that he was worried for Pat's sake because he had heard rumours that his daughter was 'knocking around with that ballad singer fella, Ronnie Drew . . . a great singer, I grant you, but a desperate gurrier'. I assured him that he was misinformed, that Ronnie's persona as a professional ballad singer was misleading, and that, while not perhaps a daily communicant, he was an artist held in high regard and a decent chap. My own reputation must have been still relatively untarnished because the worried party was much relieved. Whether he briefed Ronnie's prospective father-in-law and what reply he might have got I know not.

My longest connection with Ronnie, professionally, on a one-to-one basis, was in a show called *The Bells of Hell*, in which I played Brendan Behan performing bits and pieces from his own works, while Ronnie sang the musical link pieces and some solo items, one of which was a ballad he wasn't familiar with. As guitar players the world over have done since forever, he pasted the words of the new song on the back of his guitar.

On the first night, in the presence of no less a person than the drama critic of the *Irish Independent*, Ronnie swept on stage, and as he passed my narrator's chair his prompt sheet detached itself from its position and fluttered to my feet. Halfway through the first verse he pushed the guitar forward from his belly to consult the prompt sheet. Before he could panic, proud as a boy scout, I covered his agony by picking up the next line and completing the verse. By the divine rule that no good deed should go unpunished, the Indo man, lynx-eyed pro that he was, wrote acidly, 'Mr Toibin should leave the singing – all of it – to Mr Drew.'

'Fuck you, Mr Drew, and your mates in the Indo,' I not only thought but said.

Whilst our relationship was not turbulent – except of course when it was – we recognized each other's shortcomings. Once, after a severe mauling from a rural audience much sustained by liquor, Ronnie was discussing the evening's doing with the owner of the elegant cow-byre that passed for a venue.

'And ye do shows with Niall Toibin, I believe?' said the proprietor.

'Yes,' said Ronnie.

'I'd like to have him here. Would he be dear?'

'You'd have to negotiate with his manager.'

'Oh. Aye. How long would he do?'

'Ye mean here?'

'Aye.'

'About three minutes, I'd say.'

There is very little new to be said of The Dubliners. John Sheahan is remembered as the non-wandering son. As is Barney. Ciarán, Luke and even Ronnie came and went or in their turn simply went. And yet the band retained its potency. Ronnie in particular remained the quintessential Dubliner. (Showbiz-wise, that is. Of course, we all know he was an adopted Dub; wasn't he really from Dunleary or the Noggin or somewhere?)

I recall a fund-raiser for the SDLP in the National Stadium in their cradle days when their title allowed all the southern parties to claim affinity with them. Richard Harris was the big draw, though I can't recall what he did on the night. I recited Rabbie Burns's 'A man's a man for a' that'. God knows why.

Then The Dubliners took the stage – the real, genuine, fourteen-carat, original, Dubliners – Ronnie, Luke, Barney, John and Ciarán. Where the roof landed was anybody's guess. Dick Burke of Fine Gael (well, then, anyway) remarked to me, 'They're very good, of course, The Dubliners. Everybody loves them. But I must admit their songs have a populist tinge that doesn't impinge on my range of sensibilities.' When in due course I conveyed this reaction to Ronnie, he said, 'Jaze, we'll have to do somethin' about that – like find out what it means.'

His demeanour backstage could belie his public image. He could be sick with nerves, quite a worrier. I can still recall my own astonishment at how, in the few short steps from the wings to the footlights, his anxious expression was transformed into the challenging delivery of that deadly diapason that left no room for ambiguity or fudge.

Folly that with your performin' seals.

PART 3

Starting over

I had huge admiration for him when he left The Dubliners the last time. I really thought it was the best thing he could have done. But in actual fact it was almost like starting all over again and this was at the age of sixty-two. It was almost like going back to the drawing board.

Phelim, October 2008

When I started the album [*Dirty Rotten Shame*] I had no intentions of leaving the band. It didn't come into my head at all. I just thought I'd make a solo album and that'd be it. But then I found I had a lot of freedom when making this record . . . I immediately had the support of my family, my wife, my son and daughter, and that really made me feel that whatever the outcome, this would be a very healthy thing for me to do.

Dubliners Magazine, 1996

I don't feel particularly brave. I consider it normal to try to progress and do different things. People who think that's brave are people who may have given up or something. It's easy to get in a rut. I don't know how long I'll last, but neither does someone who is forty-five.

Irish Music, October 1997

You know this security thing that you'd always get thrown at you. By everybody. By the whole society. I don't have security even now. But then again, I don't miss it because I never had it. It's a way of life for me not to have security. At the same time, I don't have a whingeing attitude of I wish I had it . . . I was in a pub here about a year ago

Ronnie announced that Keith Donald (right), formerly of Moving Hearts,
would manage him when he went solo at the end of 1995.

with a friend of my son's. We went down to see a band playing. And
when it was over I said to yer man, 'I'm getting out of this place. It's
full of 45-year-old auld fellas.' Fellas in their middle forties and that
was it: they were having their three pints. They weren't actually
smoking pipes, but they were metaphorically smoking their pipes.
Whereas I've met old guys in the country and old guys in Dublin and
they'd be eighty but they still have a bit of devilment or a bit of
something. And there's a great presumption about people looking for
security because they presume they're going to live to be eighty or
ninety. I never presumed I'd live. I didn't think I'd last this long.

Sunday Independent, February 1998

I always wanted my children to do whatever made them happy, which
is not to say I didn't care and I probably had a moment when I wanted
Phelim to be a solicitor, but not for the poshness, but for to give me
a dig-out.

Sunday Independent, July 2004

Ronnie and Phelim in Rome,
Christmas 1996

We had a ball that Christmas. Cliodhna was feeling the need to spend
Christmas with David's parents and then my girlfriend at the time
was saying it would be nice if we spent Christmas on our own this
year. Myself and Cliodhna had talked Mam and Dad into going away
for Christmas rather than being at home on their own. And they were
excited about the trip. In the meantime myself and the girlfriend went
our separate ways and then when I was on my own for Christmas
they invited me along. It turned out to be great. I remember one night
– Dad wasn't drinking but I wanted to go for a pint – we went for a
walk down some of the back streets and Dad always had a great nose
for good places, good local spots that wouldn't be where the tourists
would go, and we found this little bar, and Dad said, I bet we'll have
a bit of crack in here. And he was right.

Phelim, October 2008

I'd been saying I was going to leave for a while. I wanted to do
something different, something on my own, but when you're drinking
to the extent that I was, you make all these plans, you say you're

In June 1997 President Mary Robinson hosted a Family Day at Áras an Uachtaráin, with Ronnie as the star attraction. Afterwards his party were photographed with the president. His mother, Peg Drew, took pride of place beside the president. 'She was really good at that, at taking her pride of place, she really was, wherever she was.' – Cliodhna. At the back Ronnie's sister Margie O'Brien, Ruth and Anto Drennan (guitarist), his sister Joan Byrne, Nicolas Robinson, David Dunne and Cliodhna, Lorraine and Tom O'Brien (sound engineer) and Deirdre

A typical scene in Ronnie and Deirdre's front room. This time the occasion was a visit by American cousins of Deirdre's. Ruaidhrí Dunne watches his granddad, and Phelim is the guitarist on the right.

going to do this, that and the other, and then you go on the batter again and put it all on the long finger – you know, put it off, let things slide – and I'd just end up staying where I was. But ever since I stopped I've been able to focus on things much better, and with greater energy than before, which gave me the impetus finally to get on with it.

Scotland on Sunday, August 1998

Another typical scene in the Drews, where visitors were welcomed with open arms. Ronnie's brother Gerry, actor Charlie Roberts, Carroll Preston (whose wife was an old friend of Deirdre) and Ronnie

Carroll was a Northern Presbyterian and when he'd get a few jars in him he'd put a bucket on his head, a scarf across him and a brush upside-down and he'd do the lads marching on the 12th on the way up and then marching back pissed. It was a great little act he had. Actually, he died here, one night, at a party. Everybody except for my mother and I were rotten and my friend Fiona Fortune (who's also since dead) was a nurse. She wasn't qualified at the time, and she broke two of his ribs, but she brought him back to life. The ambulance men came in and they thought they'd entered a lunatic asylum and they put Carroll in a chair and wrapped him in a blanket and strapped him in. But he left singing, 'It is old, but it is beautiful . . .' and waving his arm.

Cliodhna, October 2008

Ronnie's show, Ronnie, I Hardly Knew Ya!, *opened in July 1997. It and its successor*, An Evening with Ronnie Drew, *continued to tour nationally and internationally until the mid-2000s. His colleague in the show and his performing partner for that decade was his friend, former Stockton's Wing member Mike Hanrahan. 'I always give Mike his dues. He took on a lot of responsibilities with Dad. Mike took on organizing flights and hotels and all that stuff and making sure Dad was all right. He was always very good to him.' – Phelim*

The media were exceptionally good to me in the sense that I got great reviews for the show in every newspaper. That was something that I didn't expect. I was very gratified. I didn't make any money out of the show. I've been doing one thing for so many years that now I've changed over I suppose it's understandable that people are kind of wondering. And I can understand that. But nevertheless I know it's successful, even though I didn't make any money. When I say I didn't make any money out of it, I paid the rent. The reason I would like to make a few bob out of it is that it gives you freedom; it gives you time, so you don't have to be running out and doing a gig in some unsuitable place.

Sunday Independent, February 1998

With Joan Baez in Holland in 1995

The pitch is perfect, the diction impeccable and the interpretations virtually unique. His recitations have the same quality, whether he is immersed in some of James Joyce's more irreverent poems or a generous extract from an O'Casey play. His feeling for the words, and indeed for the authors, is absolutely right, and gives them added value

199

... Those unfamiliar with Ronnie Drew as a solo act may be surprised at his easy dominance and will surely revel in it. He is a class act.

Irish Times, July 1997

Lyrics would be my thing. I love good poetry and good writing. I wouldn't be describing myself as well read, but I've read a lot of stuff. Sometimes I feel a responsibility to read because I wasted so much time when I was drinking in the early part of my life. I didn't waste as much as a lot of people I know, but I wasted too much for my comfort.

Daily Telegraph, August 1998

I met these people that I hadn't seen in a while and it was, 'Hello, Ronnie, what are you having?' And I had only been a fairly short time off the drink. I didn't have any craving for drink or anything. 'No, I won't have anything.' And the temptation is always there to say, 'I have a pain in me stomach,' or 'I'm on tablets,' or something. But that means the problem is ongoing. And they kept on saying, 'Why won't you have a drink? Why?' 'I'm just not having anything.' And eventually somebody piped up: 'Well, I saw you at a wedding one time . . .' And I thought, 'It's all going to come out now, whatever I did at the wedding.' So I thought, 'I'm starting to feel very negative about this.' If there's any negative feeling around I give it to those who are creating it. So I said: 'Well, the fact is that I'm an alcoholic and if I start to drink I mightn't stop.' And then they got embarrassed. So actually what I did was I turned it all around and I found it was a good lesson in ordinary life as well. That if you're up-front then it's gone and there can be no more whispering in the corner.

Sunday Independent, February 1998

[on including Christy Moore's 'Viva la Quinta Brigada' on *Dirty Rotten Shame*]: Christy had often said to me that he thought this song would suit me, and I have a great affection for Christy. And not just affection, but a great respect for him, and for all he's done. So if Christy makes a suggestion, I listen to it carefully. And this is a very good song, because it really lays the blame where it's due . . . This is another song that I could have done with The Dubliners. I still have a great passion for this sort of music. It's part of my life and always will be, I guess.

Irish Music, October 1995

Years ago they called people like me reds, the worst thing you could be. If you were getting near to finding out how the government was on the fiddle you were called a red. Now they've got a new word. They call you a cynic. Well, I am a cynic and fucking proud of it.

Sunday Times, June 2000

I'm fed up hearing how we'll lose all the wealth we've gained over the last few years if we don't keep people's wages down. It's just the same old story of getting people to work for nothing.

Irish Examiner, March 2005

The worst stage Irishness that I see is this kind of trying to present the Irish as 'Ah, we're all very nice people.' We're not all nice people. We have our ups and our downs, our goods and our bads, y'know . . . Stage Irishness to me is trying to present this image. The government do it a lot [when they] say that we are all nice people here, that we won't tell anyone to fuck off, that we put up with all this shite, don't complain about the government and agree that Europe is a great place to be in. That's stage Irishness as far as I'm concerned. We're not like that.

In Dublin, August 1992

I hear people going on about café lattes and cappuccinos as if they're the greatest things. Half these people don't know what they're talking about. We were drinking café lattes years ago travelling around the world and we just accepted it was coffee . . . I don't feel the need to please or impress anybody, which is a great feeling. My friends and family still put up with me, which is all that matters.

Evening Herald, April 2002

They needed to cast the skipper of the ship in the episode, and I was sitting beside Owen Roe and the director was talking to Owen and next thing Owen said, 'Well, Phelim will probably have the very man

Michael O'Riordan, Ronnie and Fr Austin Flannery at Michael
O'Riordan's eightieth birthday party at Liberty Hall, November 1997.
Michael O'Riordan, founder of the Communist Party of Ireland, was a
survivor of the 15th International Brigade celebrated in Christy Moore's
song 'Viva la Quinta Brigada'.

Ronnie and Phelim featured in the BBC TV series The Ambassador *in July*
1998. Playing skipper of an Irish trawler, Ronnie got to say: 'I'm arresting
youse for piracy in Irish waters,' to the crew of a British Navy frigate.

for you.' And the director said, 'I'm looking for the skipper for the ship – a big beard and so on.' And I said, 'It might seem like nepotism, but, if you didn't mind, my dad'd probably be the best man for that.' The gas thing is that when Dad was on the trawler they used as his boat he became great friends with the guys who ran it – this was in Balbriggan – and he ended up coming back to play at one of the young fella's weddings.

Phelim, October 2008

In 2000 Ronnie had a part in an award-winning short film, Finbar Lebowitz. *He played Mr Abramsky, a Jewish bookseller in Dublin, who mentors the film's hero, Finbar, when he converts to Judaism.*

I wouldn't call myself an actor or a singer for that matter, just a journeyman. I'll do whatever's going. I feel I must have a talent somewhere for doing something but I'm still not terribly sure what it is. I suppose it's a talent for being myself.

Sunday Times, June 2000

Ronnie at the Chelsea Hotel in Manhattan

He was delighted to tell this story. He was walking down a street in New York one day and he had on a full-length double-breasted overcoat, and the suit on underneath, and the Spanish shoes and a crisp white shirt and he was smoking a cigar. And he said he was just walking along, minding his own business, looking around, and the next thing there was these two real Italian New York guys sitting at a table and he overheard one of them saying to the other, 'Must be some kind of don, or somethin'.'

Phelim, October 2008

Three very tired Drew brothers, Gerry, Ronnie and Tony, two days after Phelim's wedding at Kinnitty Castle in 2000. 'Dad said, I can't wait to go home, put the feet up and just watch the ads.' – Phelim

In 2002 Ronnie was awarded the Irish Post's *Lifetime Achievement Award. Pictured with the family at the dinner in London is their friend Gloria McGowran.*

He loved getting awards. There was this Variety Club of Ireland Award that he got one year. It started off that he was joking about it, 'Fucking auld thing – ah, it's for charity, sure we'll go along anyway. If you're around maybe come along.' And then by the time the night came, the whole family were coming and we all had to dress up and it was a big deal. 'Ah now, it's very nice now in the end of the day to be honoured like this.'

Phelim, October 2008

In 2002 The Dubliners celebrated their fortieth anniversary, and Ronnie and Jim McCann returned to the group for the fortieth anniversary tour. President Mary McAleese hosted a reception for Dubliner members – past and present – and their families in the Áras.

If there's one thing I've learned it's to keep trying, to never give in to despair, and keep hoping. And to keep improving on things. I keep trying, whether it's music, songs or golf. I'm not very good at golf but I go out and enjoy it . . . Keep working and getting annoyed at things: that's what keeps me going.

Evening Herald, April 2002

Guitarist Anto Drennan's daughters Regan and Olivia watch as Ronnie and Deirdre cut the cake celebrating their fortieth wedding anniversary.

Ronnie in the kitchen at the party celebrating his fortieth wedding anniversary

The scene in the kitchen at the fortieth wedding celebration. Among the guests are BP Fallon (at the cupboard doors), Ronnie's Italian collaborator, Antonio Breschi (second right of BP Fallon), and other long-time friends and musical associates Clive Collins (in the middle of the floor with the fiddle) and Donal McDonald (bottom-left-hand corner).

Mam and Dad could fight like cats and dogs but they didn't fight like cats and dogs over mundane things – I remember, say, in the early days, in my youth, when my dad's drinking would maybe get out of hand, that my mother would confront him about it. And that's when I remember quite colourful arguments. In that way they could fight like cats and dogs like any couple. But in general my mother could be quite short with my dad if he was displaying this quality that he had for getting other people to do things for him. My dad could be hopeless sometimes. There'd be something there, close by, and he'd sort of say, 'Deirdre would you get that,' or 'Phelim, get that thing.' Or he'd get himself into a state looking for something that would be under a paper under his nose, but he wouldn't bother his arse looking hard enough, waiting for somebody to find it. And that's where my mother would just completely lose it. It wouldn't be one thing, it would be a couple of things. 'Oh, for fuck's sake, Ronnie.' Joe Ó Broin, who was a great friend of Dad's, he used to do a great impression of my mother. 'Oh, for fuck's sake, Ronnie' when she'd be giving out to him. And it wouldn't be because he was on the phone chewing the arse off somebody – that was just Ronnie dealing with things the way he dealt with them – but if I gave out to somebody, or Cliodhna, she'd be down on us like a ton of bricks; he was different.

When she was about four my niece, Aoife, got a report card for her play-group, and I thought this was hilarious, and Cliodhna was showing me the report card and it came from the head of the little school she was in and it said, 'Aoife is a lovely chid. She is very warm and friendly with all the other kids and mixes easily. However, she has this knack of getting other people to do things for her, which they do gladly.' We were all thinking at the time, 'Jesus, she didn't lick it up off a stone.'

Phelim, October 2008

There is no secret to my long marriage. It's just a question of keeping going. I suppose luck had something to do with it.

Sunday Independent, May 2004

When the last of the aunts died, they left the house to my mum and dad. I think they shared out quite a lot of the proceeds to the rest of the family, but they decided it would be prudent to put the larger portion of it into a business, a flower shop. Unfortunately, they weren't experienced. It didn't work out and it was an awful shame, because I think it was meant as a means to provide an income for Mam and Dad into their old age, a source of steady money coming in, but unfortunately it didn't work out.

There might have been a time for about six months of feeling a bit sorry for themselves, and rightly so when you plough a few bob into something and it goes belly-up. But then after that they sort of said, 'Ah well sure, nothing ventured, nothing gained.'

And then, as the years went by, when he wasn't drinking it was only necessary to have the money for basic necessities – the house was paid for, the car, a few cigars, the odd dinner. He did find a sort of contentment in those years and that definitely fed through right up until the end. There were times when he got a bit out of control with the gargle but he knew himself well enough to get that back under control and knew that if he wanted to be able to enjoy the few jars that he had to keep it under control and he couldn't revert to the way he had been before when he went on binges.

Phelim, October 2008

There were periods in my life when I didn't have any money but I never worried too much about it. Something always turns up and, in those days, you could go down to the local bank manager, who would give you a few bob when you needed it. I had two good bank managers, Mr Condon and Mr Bride, and I could always go to them if I was short of a few bob. There was none of that 'terms and conditions apply' rubbish, as it was all done on a personal basis. They always trusted me.

I'm a spender. I like to buy cigars, go to restaurants and go to the theatre. I don't smoke all that much – two or three a day. I bring cigars back from Spain if I've been on holiday or friends bring them for me. I like to eat in restaurants when I'm in Spain, France or Italy. When I'm at home I like to eat out too, but I steer clear of any place that's fashionable. I like to go to a place with straightforward food where there is a nice crowd of people. Not those places that put coconut milk and lemongrass in everything, even on a leg of lamb.

Sunday Times, March 2006

Dad used to get cigars in Spain or if somebody was coming over they'd bring him over a couple of hundred. It was much cheaper than buying them here. It didn't work out any more expensive than my mother's cigarette-smoking – he worked it out. But she claimed he smoked more than he reckoned he did. And he smoked very, very heavily after she died.

Cliodhna, October 2008

The genius of Drew's performance lies in its lack of flourishes; his charm is that of the genuine article. In his way, Kavanagh was right. Ronnie Drew is trying to fool the people – but the people can see the brilliance behind his gruff, low-key demeanour.

Irish Echo, March 2004

Eleanor [Shanley] and Dad had a lovely relationship. Eleanor has such a lovely way about her. And he had good relationships with women in general, people like Gloria McGowran, Eleanor, Mary Troy, who's an academic. He had a lot of time for a lot of different women. Maybe it was being brought up by a houseful of women.

I think he was exceptional because he was a mass of contradictions. While he would be a man's man in many respects, he'd also be very protective towards people who were more sensitive. And he wouldn't have any hang-ups about people who were of different sexual persuasions. He'd be as happy in the company of gay men, lesbian women – he didn't give a shite who you were, or what your sexual preference was, or where you came from, as long as you could hold your own in conversation.

Phelim, October 2008

Ronnie hosted a celebratory eightieth birthday lunch for journalist and broadcaster Seán Mac Réamoinn in 2002, and he used it as an opportunity to catch up with friends from every part of his life. It was a huge affair, upstairs in Dobbins Restaurant in Dublin.

Seán Mac Réamoinn and Deirdre

Phelim and Mike Hanrahan

June Levine, Ivor Browne and Ronnie

With his old friend from the Telephone Exchange, John Kelly

Ciarán MacMathúna and Frank Harte

Eamonn Campbell and Barney McKenna

Louis Stewart, John Sheahan and Jim McCann

In 2006 Ronnie recorded an album with Eleanor Shanley,
El Amor De Mi Vida (The Love of My Life).

A whole new departure for Ronnie at seventy – as a DJ
at Death Disco in Dublin, Christmas 2004
(see BP Fallon's piece, page 225)

I find Shane to be a most sensitive person, a poet. I'm not caught up in all that's said about him and the drink. I mean, he drinks, but it's his own fucking business.

Sunday Independent, February 2005

Life now is less frenetic, less hale and hearty. Back then it was fast and furious living, all parties and drinking and shouting. In our hotel last night there was a lad, locked, asleep on one of the couches in the corridor and I thought to myself, 'Ah yeah, I too have lived.' And you know, I don't miss any of that carry on.

An Evening with Ronnie Drew, Geneva, programme notes, April 2005

An unusual sight, Ronnie fishing. 'He got a loan of those runners off somebody anyway. They weren't his.' – Phelim

Ronnie was delighted to be grand marshal of Dublin's St Patrick's Day Parade in 2006. He is shown here at the door of the Dining Hall in Trinity College, at the VIP breakfast prior to the parade.

Fintan O'Toole: For funny, engaging, entertaining and absorbing as it is, *An Evening with Ronnie Drew* is also a chance to encounter a genuine national treasure. Anyone over forty will relish the chance to meet one of the genuine heroes of Irish popular culture in such an intimate setting. Anyone under forty should go along to learn that even without Elvis we had our own rock and roll.

Irish Times, March 2005

In August 2006 Ronnie had his handprints cast in bronze for permanent display at the plaza outside Dublin's Gaiety Theatre. He is pictured here with his grandchildren: Cliodhna's son and daughter, Ruaidhrí and Aoife, and Phelim's sons, Vivian (in the buggy) and Milo.

Apart from staying alive, truth is the most important thing in this life. You can't always be truthful. But as long as you're not telling lies to yourself, you're OK.

Sunday Independent, May 2004

Wisdom is not a natural thing that comes. You have to have been paying attention to your life. Some people don't pay attention and they never acquire any wisdom. I wouldn't say it's wisdom, but certainly down through the years I have reviewed my opinions and I haven't just accepted what I believed when I was twenty. I only know that when I was twenty-six or twenty-seven I knew everything and now I don't know quite so much.

Living It, July/August 2006

We had it all

Mike Hanrahan

We had it all
We had the best of times
We had a life that dreams are made of.

I wrote 'We Had It All' in 1994 to mark the end of a fourteen-year roller-coaster ride with Stockton's Wing. For some reason I wanted Ronnie to record the song with me so I called him and, true to form, he obliged. We recorded in Dublin along with Stockton's Wing friends Peter Keenan, Maurice Lennon, Paul Roche, Robbie Casserly and my brother Kieran. Looking back now, that recording session represents a major personal and professional bridge in my life.

I got to know Ronnie as an entertainer in childhood. My dad,

Jackie, had a few Dubliners LPs and when I listened to the music there was always something about Ronnie Drew's voice: humour, authority, a bit of 'devilment'. And on many songs the voice itself was the great messenger, and as a messenger Ronnie got your attention whichever way and however he needed: telling us about McAlpine's men in London, the party at Finnegan's Wake, or describing the horror of Gallipoli and the scorn and irreverence poured on the returning walking wounded . . .

Years later, on stage at Andrew's Lane Theatre in Dublin, working with Ronnie in his one-man show, I would sometimes close my eyes and be briefly transported to my parents' house and then return to the stage and look over to my left to watch Ronnie perform to my guitar accompaniment. On those occasions I thought 'my life cannot get any better' . . . but of course it did and we travelled through a few continents with the show.

From the early eighties a very solid friendship developed between Stockton's Wing and The Dubliners. We toured together, shared many festival bills and a good few bottles as well. It was wild at times but always fun and we enjoyed hours of music sessions. I even remember a session at a German airport after missing a flight. The music was always good with The Dubs and the craic was mighty.

In 1997 Ronnie called and asked me to help him out with his new show. I was more than interested and I knew it was going to be a great experience. The show forced me to concentrate and work hard on my guitar skills, and I will always be thankful to him for that. He might laugh but I know he made me a decent guitarist. He set a very high performance standard and I relished the challenge.

Ronnie always described *Ronnie, I Hardly Knew Ya!* as 'a one-man show I'm doing with Mike Hanrahan'. It sounded good to me and very Ronnie. He was an inclusive man yet always aware that his name adorned the poster. The business was something that had to be done – recordings, interviews, TV appearances, handshakes, autographs, photographs, and so on – but the theatre show was very different. He cherished and respected those associated with the show – lighting, stage and sound crews and, of course, the musicians. He was most comfortable in that company: talking shop, telling stories or giving out about music business 'heads', politicians or some TV and radio personalities.

Life on the road with Ronnie was a rare experience. He introduced me to some very interesting people and we both connected on many levels. I cannot recall any serious falling out; we laughed regularly, talked a lot, yet we allowed each other the space to maintain our sanity during intense periods of work. And we shared a preference for good food and hotels.

In Ronnie's mind Ireland was changing rapidly with the Celtic Tiger rolling along, and I know he felt we were losing some of our heart and soul to the boom. He used to say the only thing the Celtic Tiger did for him was get in his way, with all the road works, traffic chaos and building going on all over the country. The theatre show allowed him to keep a snapshot of an Ireland not long ago. Hotels, his second home, were being taken over by major chains; personality was set aside and service gave way to margins. He lamented the disintegration of the service industry: the passing of tea rooms in favour of fast-food joints; the proliferation of paper cups, plastic knives, cheap carveries and the ubiquity of the dreaded microwave. He suspected that Dublin Bay prawns were probably from Taiwan and Limerick ham had never tasted the green pastures of east Limerick.

On the road the dressing room was his haven and always private, strictly for the performers and crew. One night after the show a theatre lady charged into the dressing room to inquire if we needed anything. At that point Ronnie's trousers were at his ankles and he turned and walked towards her to say, in colourful language, that all he needed was a little time to change his trousers and would she . . . well you can imagine. The poor woman froze solid and had to be asked a second time to leave.

When we played in Israel I managed to persuade Ronnie to take a bus to Jerusalem. Ronnie was never a good tourist but he agreed. His mum was very ill in Dublin at the time and I think he saw the trip to the Holy City as a diversion. We went by bus. It was a two-hour journey full of locals and fresh Israeli Army conscripts with rifles and all the trimmings. Throughout the day his grey beard and dark suit brought a lot of attention, with people saluting and bowing in reverence. I said, 'Even in Israel, Ronnie, you are a star.' We laughed about that for a long time. We saw all the holy spots and ended up at the Wailing Wall. The scene fascinated me: so many people, the strange movements, the hum of prayer. I was taking it all in when Ronnie called to me, 'Mikey, what time does it change colour?'

I said naively, 'It doesn't change colour, Ronnie.'

'Well, it's just a wall, then, Mike, and we've seen it, so can we get back to the hotel now?'

As a man Ronnie was old-fashioned in so many ways and his domestic role was extremely limited: Deirdre was always there to sort it out. Deirdre was the quintessential lady – beautiful, strong, supportive and a very loving person. And she carried out many roles: wife, mother, grandmother, secretary, editor, reader, listener to first drafts and ideas, and constant companion to so many of us who passed by. She was a rock of good counsel and great to share a bit of gossip, lots of laughter and plenty of tea, coffee and sweet things.

Deirdre was a regular at the live shows and on occasion she would tell Ronnie stories, such as the time when she insisted that Ronnie mow the lawn and he finally agreed. When he finished he asked Deirdre who he should return the lawnmower to; she informed him that it had been in their possession for five years. She loved telling that one. Or the time when dogs were soiling the front garden. Ronnie threatened to erect a sign at the front gate: ' Dogs . . . beware of the owner'. She was a great woman, sophisticated, with a great dress sense. I think she gave a lot of that to Ronnie. Ronnie was always well groomed and appearance was important, no matter what the occasion.

Ronnie's one-man show was the centre of his professional life during my ten years or so as his guitarist, writer, producer, tour manager and friend. It was an incredible production that showcased his deep love and respect for literature, poetry, songs and a good yarn. During that time we also produced four albums. Later I was music director on the *Eleanor Shanley/Ronnie Drew Show*. They made a brilliant combination: an ageing Dublin balladeer and a much younger trad singer from a farm in Leitrim. They played on that and enjoyed the experience, as we all did, and the audience were so much the better for the voices, the stage antics and the songs chosen. We all worked hard to develop and produce a great show, and it was easy because Ronnie and Eleanor had mutual affection and respect for each other's person-alities and craft, and a dedication to the show. There was something in the air on that stage with Ronnie and Eleanor, and the great Steven Flaherty and myself on guitars.

Soon after Ronnie was diagnosed, Deirdre called to say she thought he might not perform again. It was devastating news, and, after spend-ing a long time considering my future, I decided to leave the music industry and pursue a career as a chef and enrolled in the Ballymaloe Cookery School. During my studies Ronnie would call me regularly to see how I was progressing. As a dedicated foodie himself I know he was happy for me. We would chat on about the music and tour plans, and if we talked about the business he would say, 'You are probably better off out of the business now. It's changing fast.'

Ronnie wished me nothing but well on my new road and that meant a lot to me. Despite his illness we still managed a few gigs. I will treasure those along with the countless wonderful experiences we shared together.

Such a pity now that Ireland's cultural landscape has lost one of its treasures. Such a pity too that a lot of us have lost a good friend and companion. He was a powerful man and Deirdre was an inspirational woman. I am all the better for their friendship.

The last verse of 'We Had It All' was my dad's favourite. The song is the thread that has spun through my life and times spent with Ronnie:

> There's a sailor gone to sea, only he knows how it feels
> as he bids a fond farewell to all his kin
> as he walks along the shore to his love he throws a rose
> I'll return again in winter or in spring.
>
> We had it all
> We had the best of times
> We had a life that dreams are made of.

Where the sun meets the sky
a soldier standing by
his eyes they cannot hide that lonesome tale
threre's a photograph of home, the smell of sweet cologne
and words of love forever and a day.

We had it all
We had the best of times
We had a life that dreams are made of.

At the station she boards a train, wet with tears and rain
and a father holds a mother's empty hand
all the things you need to know, she whispers as she goes
what I have I hold forever in my heart.

We had it all
We had the best of times
We had a life that dreams are made of.

On an old country lane where the wilderness still reigns
an old man takes a flower in his hand
Well, I've watched you bloom and fade
All the beauty you create
I'll take this pleasure with me as we part.

We had it all
We had the best of times
We had a life that dreams are made of.

Ronnie Drew's most surreal gigs ever!

When Ronnie Drew became a disc jockey at Death Disco

BP Fallon

'This is great, isn't it?' Ronnie Drew shoots at you out the side of his mouth, adding, 'As you'd say yourself, this is the vibe!'

It certainly is.

The man is beaming. He never did this crazy craic before. Done most everything but . . . our DJ Ronnie Drew spinning CDs to an adoring audience in a New York rock 'n' roll club . . . well, this is a new one for the books.

It's St Patrick's Night 2004 in The Big Apple and the debut in

America of Death Disco – the rock 'n' roll party run by yourself and the fêted Scottish rock mogul Alan McGee, aka 'The Man Who Discovered Oasis'. The name of the party, it's more dark humour than morbid, coming from the title of a song written by John Lydon, aka Johnny Rotten. The party's slogan is 'Death Disco: Life's a Gas'.

And now as his wife Deirdre watches from the wings with a smile on her face that says 'God, would you ever look at him now!' there's Ronnie, sober of suit and manner, grey of hair and beard and grinning a grin from here to China, his eyes twinkling as he dances on stage not only with gusto but with fellow DJ Jaime Coon. Miss Coon, she's dressed only in black knickers and – to celebrate the night that's in it – green glitter in the shape of a shamrock over each nipple. Glorious madness.

And in between shaking a tailfeather the admirable Mr Drew kicks off on the decks with Rory Gallagher, followed by The Dubliners and The Pogues united to sing 'The Irish Rover'. He announces each song into the microphone, explains its significance. He plays Thin Lizzy in tribute to Phil Lynott, includes 'Sweet Thing' by Van Morrison ('a friend and a man I admire'), then says into the mic, 'Here's a song written by an Irishman who used to be my neighbour . . . Jimmy Kennedy,' and spins the scorching 'Red Sails in the Sunset' by Dinah Washington.

The great Ronnie Drew finishes his eclectic set by noting, 'Here's a song written by Brendan Behan. This is a song I've been associated with but this time it's not by me. "The Auld Triangle" by Bob Dylan,' and the venue is quelled as this unreleased treasure from *The Basement Tapes* floods the room. Incredible. The track ends and suddenly the quieted venue bursts into an explosion of applause and Ronnie bows, still grinning like a Cheshire cat.

And as he and Deirdre make their way back into the snowy New York night, Mr Drew is engulfed by new fans. 'I'm from Texas,' says a young guy in a Clash t-shirt. 'Loved your set. Where else do you DJ, sir?'

The answer comes in Dublin. It's now Christmas 2004 and we're at the Death Disco Dublin XXXmas Party. The stage is dressed in yuletide folly, a white Christmas tree on one side of the decks and a white

Christmas, um, shrub on the other. Lights twinkle as from the Death Disco banner the punk rock icons The Ramones gaze down at the DJ altar. This Christmas party's a cracker. You've played a few tunes, the place is stuffed, the joint is jumpin', the dancefloor's pumpin'. Ah, the freedom to rock!

DJ transmogrifies into MC as you trumpet, 'The Godfather of Irish Music, The Rock of Ages!' and here's Ronnie Drew in an immaculate suit, Death Disco XXXmas Party badge in his lapel. Ronnie's appearance on stage behind the decks is greeted by the multitude like something akin to a holy experience but a rockin' one, as if Little Richard is conducting the service with whoops and hollers and cries of jubilation.

Even Ronnie, who's been on stage for well over fifty years, is taken aback at this wild reception. Hands aloft, he basks in the love and the warmth from the crowd before DJ Ronnie Drew whacks out Them roaring through 'Please Don't Go' and The Kinks' pop punk metal guitar cruncher 'You Really Got Me' before telling us he's going to play a song he recorded 'with a friend of mine, Rory Gallagher' and the gears go even higher as Ronnie sings into the mic over his own voice alongside Rory's on their 'Barley and Grape Rag'. Mighty. Janis Joplin is next for the Ronnie Drew duo treatment, his gravelly voice just perfect with her battered blues smile through Kristofferson's 'Me and Bobby McGee' and now the room is joining in, 'Freedom's just another word for nothin' left to lose'. It could've been gank. It's beyond brilliant.

And another masterstroke: Ronnie plays a track by his old group The Dubliners, 'Whiskey in the Jar', and everyone's singing along and then the crafty Mr Drew segues it into Thin Lizzy's rocked-up 'Whiskey in the Jar' – Eric Bell's guitar intro, Lizzy's first-ever hit, the song Phil Lynott had learnt from The Dubliners. Magic. The audience goes nuts.

And the crowd roars again as Ronnie Drew climaxes with the rambunctious sound of 'The Irish Rover' by The Dubliners joined by their musical godchildren The Pogues and once more Ronnie's deep dark voice sings over his own on the record, duetting now with Shane MacGowan's vocal on the track and on cue DJ Shane MacGowan makes his grand showbiz entrance, fingers held in the air in some reverse Churchillian gesture.

Shane, he plays everything from Margaret Barry to The Sex Pistols via Led Zeppelin, Dylan and Joy Division. Shane too, he often sings over the CDs he's playing.

And both Ronnie Drew and Shane MacGowan in their separate sets play Brendan Bowyer & The Royal Showband's 1964 Irish smash 'The Hucklebuck'. It wasn't a very good record and it was a great one. In his fruity tremulous warble young Brendan Bowyer, Ireland's homegrown Elvis from Waterford, had urged everyone to do the hucklebuck, his laddish grin suggesting this was the route to fun and girls meeting boys. So tonight people had wiggled like snakes and waddled like ducks and did whatever the heck they fancied, as indeed it should be.

And you and Shane hug each other, happy to be here . . . happy to be anywhere.

Not bad for a couple of old tarts DJing at the DDD XXXmas Party – plus the revered and rockin' seventy-years-young Ronnie Drew DJing and singing too with more lead in his pencil than a Faber-Castell factory.

Flash forward to 30 March 2008. You're sitting in Ronnie's kitchen in Greystones after a delicious dinner prepared by his indomitable sister Joan. Ronnie hasn't eaten much, just picked at his food. It's almost nine months since Deirdre his wife and best friend has died from cancer and Ronnie's sadness permeates his very being. It's darker than the debilitating effects of the chemo he himself is receiving in his own battle. Yes, cancer. Tough and terrible times.

And then his mood lifts and he's telling stories about the bould Barney McKenna or when he worked in the Post Office, Ronnie cracking jokes in between fierce coughing and the relighting of his recalcitrant cigar, reminiscing about when you flew with The Dubliners on a rickety old plane to the Faeroe Islands and the night in Hamburg you invited them all to the aptly named Madhouse Club.

And now he's into some narrative about some stuffy bank who wouldn't give him his own money. And one of the many beauties of this special man shines through once more as he tells of how he brought these pompous bankers to heel, fought them with intelligence and logic and humour until they gave in and gave up and gave him his few bob.

See, Ronnie Drew had great rock 'n' roll spirit. Like Johnny Cash, Ronnie Drew was a folk hero who scaled the heights but forever had the common touch. He was never tamed. He never became docile like some wagging-headed toy dog in the back of a car. He was always ready to stand up to pomposity and self-grandiose idiots. 'You're a punk rocker!' you chortle at him by way of a compliment on that Greystones kitchen Sunday evening. Ronnie, this noble man of dignity, he looks at you and laughs, then coughs, then laughs again. 'I do my best,' he says.

And now it's dateline Dublin, 27 June 2005, and we're at Death Disco's oddly named Are You Too Vertical? party – a loose pun on the U2 Vertigo tour which played in Dublin earlier that night. Shane MacGowan and you are DJing again and before Shane comes on you spin a few. Then you announce 'Anything can happen at Death Disco!' as you introduce a surprise guest, 'a man who has DJed at Death Disco in New York and at Death Disco in Dublin – the greatest living Irishman, Ronnie Drew!' and yes, it's Ronnie from The Dubliners and beyond and the audience goes bonkers. 'I'm the oldest Death Disco DJ in the world!' this living icon announces, then dedicates his first track to his old friend Phil Lynott and plays Thin Lizzy's 'The Boys

are Back in Town'. Whooosh! Then John Lennon's 'Stand By Me' and The Pogues' 'Dirty Old Town' and it's a done deal, can't do better. Ronnie Drew rocks.

The Greatest Living Irishman will never die in my heart.

The picture on p. 225 shows BP Fallon and Ronnie in a cab in New York in December 2004; the picture on p. 228 is of Ronnie DJing at Death Disco Dublin with Shane MacGowan and BP later that month; and the picture on this page is of Ronnie and BP in Death Disco Dublin in June 2005.

PART 4

The partin' glass

The christening of Phelim and Sue's sons, Vivian and Milo, in November 2006, a few weeks into Ronnie's treatment for cancer. At the back are the children's godparents: Graham Collins and Jane Begley (Sue's brother and sister), Cliodhna and Peter O'Neill.

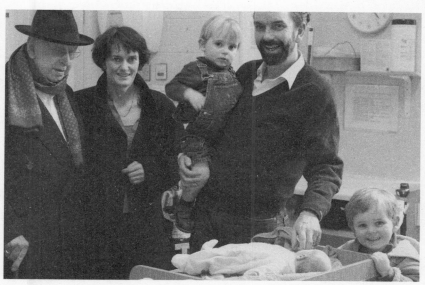

Ronnie, Cliodhna, Phelim, Milo (in Phelim's arms) and Vivian visiting Phelim and Sue's newborn twins, Seánie and Lily, February 2008

Deirdre has been a great support to me over the years and has always stood by me, not in a stand-by-your-man type of way, but I suppose she believed in the future. I don't know how she didn't kill me years ago, because if I'd been in her shoes, I would have killed me. I'm no good at sentimentality at all but neither is Deirdre – she's actually even less sentimental than I am. And I'm not one bit romantic – I can't think of anything I would like less than a candlelit dinner, or going off to Barbados – it takes fifteen shaggin' hours on an airplane.

Sunday Independent, November 2006

*A 1980s picture of Ronnie with the commissionaire of
The Dubliners' favourite hotel in Amsterdam. A rare example
of a man with hair as impressive as Ronnie's.
Ronnie always trimmed and shaped his beard himself.*

[on losing his hair]: It was my trademark. I didn't know what to do. I couldn't take it. When it started falling out I got it all shaved off. And went and bought meself a hat. I thought I was awful looking. It reminded me of – remember that fellow who used to play Nosferatu? – I felt like him. Still feel like him without the hat.

The Late Late Show, RTÉ One, December 2007

BP Fallon [on a conversation with Ronnie in 1985]: We talked about music, about Luke Kelly, who had died the year before, and Ciarán Bourke, who'd collapsed on stage from a brain haemorrhage in 1974. (He didn't mention that Ciarán was still being paid by the band, as he continued to be until his death in 1988.) Ronnie talked of Barney McKenna and John Sheahan, his other two compadres from 1962 when The Ronnie Drew Group became The Dubliners. Barney banjo-player extraordinaire, storyteller par excellence and as eccentric as a brush. John with the gliding fiddle, meticulous, organized, the only man in The Dubliners who had never taken a drink. The 'new boys' Seán Cannon and Eamonn Campbell . . . He loved them, Ronnie did, all of them, even when they drove him mad. But Deirdre was his root.

The Best of Ronnie Drew, sleeve notes, 2007

The people in the hospital were fantastic and I'd got through six sessions of treatment and I was told that the scans were proving that things had shrunken and that things were going well. And I went home and I was delighted to tell my wife. And the next day she told me that she had it. And she only lasted six weeks. I couldn't believe it. It was an awful shock. It was a dreadful loss: worst loss I've ever had.

The Late Late Show, RTÉ One, December 2007

Since I got sick last October she minded me like a baby. I was married to her for nearly forty-four years and the loss to me is incalculable. I think of the good times and now and again I think of what I should have done and what I shouldn't have done. But you can't beat yourself with a stick. You have to carry on. She was the most wonderful wife, concerned about everybody, except herself. She was a very elegant woman. She spent money on clothes like every other woman I know, but she didn't do it to look like somebody else – she did it to look like herself, and she succeeded very well. And so I carry on now and I miss her terribly. I think it was a Seán O'Casey play where he said, 'Memory is the only friend that grief can call its own.' So, of course I have great memories. As I said in the church, I was married to a lady. She was a lady always. Not always to me but to everybody else. She was always concerned about other people and when people called to the door she would invite them in instead of just handing them something at the door.

Tonight with Vincent Browne, RTÉ Radio 1, June 2007

Mary Troy [a friend from Deirdre Drew's UCD days]: What she represents to me is part of that generation that we were then, when a mortgage didn't enter your head, when you had very little money but it didn't matter because you had a great time and she saw the world like an oyster that was just there to be explored. One of her great gifts was her ability to accept everybody into the house. Anybody who came, came for maybe a weekend and three months later you'd call back and the people were still there. She was a great storyteller and she had the great gift of making everybody welcome, no matter who you were, warts and all.

Tonight with Vincent Browne, RTÉ Radio 1, June 2007

Lots of people lived with us. Joe Heaney lived with us. Seámus Ennis lived with us. A friend of my mother's whose marriage broke up, she lived with us for two years. Friends of the family. Fans from Germany sometimes arrived at the door and ended up staying over. There's always been people. And it was no big deal.

Cliodhna, October 2008

If fans said to Dad, 'We are going to Ireland on our holiday next summer,' he'd say, 'Well, if you're in Greystones, look us up.' And sometimes they did. People like Bono have big gates to keep people at bay. And I know a lot of other musicians and they're very private. My dad'd be private, but he wouldn't change his lifestyle in order to keep people at bay. Where his chair would be in the sitting room looks straight out onto the street and very often if you were in the

sitting room in Greystones people walking by would stop and have a good look in – what's going on in there? You grew to just accept it. There'd be times, I suppose as I got older, I might come out for the weekend and I'd almost want my parents to myself, and then somebody's coming to stay and you'd be like, 'Oh, Jaysus.'

My mother was just very hospitable and she would do the decent thing. If somebody was in the house and they were there for longer than an hour you offered them dinner and if they didn't go after dinner, you offered them a bed for the night. And there was a part of my mother that liked the whole thing – a bit of life in the house and something different. And very often the people who came for a cup of tea at two o'clock in the afternoon stayed until the next day, and we had great crack, and it was an excuse to get the guitar out and have a bit of fun. There was always an excuse for an impromptu night.

Phelim, October 2008

And anybody – particularly around things like Christmas – if you were on your own, you were invited.

Cliodhna, October 2008

She could handle a crisis so well. She wouldn't get upset. She knew she was dying. It obviously upset her, but everything was 'do this, do that'. She was just very brave, strong more than brave . . . She forgave an awful lot. We would have a bit of a party in the house and you would see other wives getting upset because of fellas spilling porter, but she wasn't bothered. She never drank herself, but she kept doling it out to people. She couldn't do enough for people.

Sunday Independent, August 2007

People say be positive, and you have to be positive, but it doesn't mean just saying over and over again, 'I'm going to get over this, I'm going to beat this.' That's not being positive. You have to change your whole attitude and become more – which I'm not very good at – become more tolerant. Your whole attitude has to change, I think . . . A lot of people kind of sneer at holy pictures and things, but it's all a positive energy coming your way: people are wishing you well. So no matter how kitsch it may be, it's still a positive energy coming your way. I find I accept it much more easily than I would have and I find it probably has helped me.

Saturday Night With Miriam, RTÉ One, July 2007

I haven't really a philosophy, but I try not to lose hope. You know that line over Hades, 'Abandon hope all who enter here'. I think the abandonment of hope is kind of not doing your duty. I have a duty to live, I think. And survive. You have a duty to do that, not for anybody but yourself . . . I know people are great at saying what dead people want, but I knew her very well and she was one of the bravest women I ever witnessed. It is very hard to get to know women, but after forty-four years, you get a bit of an insight . . . But she would have wished me to carry on.

Sunday Independent, August 2007

At home, in his chair in the sitting room in Greystones with Cliodhna, Phelim, Vivian and Milo, March 2008

People like to say things like, 'Oh, it really took it out of your dad when your mother died.' Of course it did. They were such a strong couple. But I think one of the things that was the huge success of their relationship was that they were always two individuals, two very strong individuals, in this partnership. While it shook him to the core when my mother died, and I don't think it did his recovery any favours, I don't think he looked at it as 'How is this affecting me now?' or 'I'm giving up' or anything like that. There were two totally different things going on. There was the grief for my mother and then there was coping with his own situation. Then, as months went by and he started to kind of find a routine that worked for him, he became a man of habit. At five o'clock he went down for his appointment in the pub and met his few pals and had his couple of glasses of wine and came home, had something to eat – or not, depending on how able he was – and then went to bed. He just followed this pattern and that's the only way he could cope after my mum went. And my Aunt Joan and Cliodhna, their reassuring presence was around all the time and they made sure he had the best of food and the best of anything that was going. I don't think Mam's passing necessarily was detrimental to his treatment.

Phelim, October 2008

It's like a part of me being gone, because I had her for so long. Like half of me gone. I really miss her so much and I wasn't expecting . . . I knew she was sick but I wasn't expecting her to go so quickly . . . I'll have to get over it but it's one of these things that it'll take me a long time to get over. Without her I wouldn't be here. I'd be gone years ago. I loved her dearly and I hope she loved me dearly. That's just the last thing to say about Deirdre.

September Song, RTÉ One, May 2008

I believe in something but I'm not quite sure what it is. The Church put a human figure on God, like the Sacred Heart, Jesus, but I don't know if Jesus is God. The Church gave us finite definitions of infinite things because our imagination only goes so far. If you're dead, you can't be judgemental. It's impossible for you to have any negative feelings, so anybody who has died can no longer be annoyed with you

Ronnie at the wedding of his niece Róisín Drew
in February 2008, along with Cliodhna and
her husband David Dunne

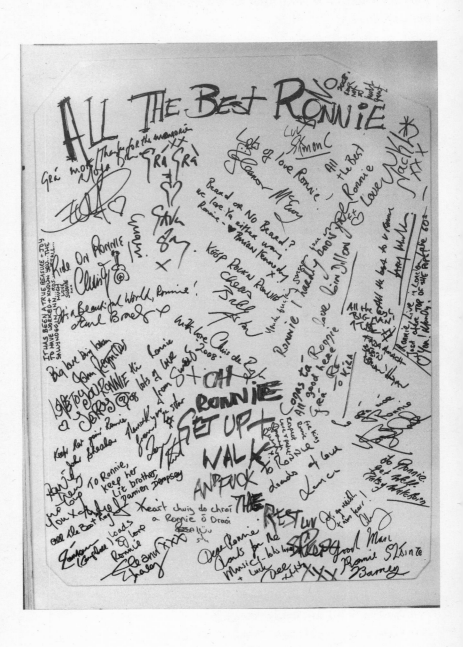

In early 2008 a gathering of Ireland's musicians recorded 'The Ballad of Ronnie Drew' as a tribute. After the recording they signed a huge card for him as follows:

Grá mór, thanks for the memories, Moya Brennan xx

Bono, 2008, your not so humble servant

Ride on, Ronnie, Christy Moore

Love, Edge

Beard or No Beard? We love ya either way, Ronnie. Love, Brian Kennedy x

Grá Grá, Gavin Friday

Keep rockin', Ronnie. Cheers, Billy (Aslan)

Guggi

It's a Beautiful World, Ronnie! Paul Brady

With love, Chris de Burgh, 2008

Big love, big man, John Reynolds

It has been a true pleasure to have worked with you and known you . . . The Sallynoggin Inn . . . RDS et al – much love, Suzanne (Doyle) xxx

Love to you, Ronnie, Jerry Fish, '08

Keep her going – John Sheahan

To Ronnie, keep her lit, brother, Damien Dempsey

Ronnie Drew, we love you, Andrea x

All the best, Eamonn (Campbell)

Loads of love, Ronnie, Eleanor Shanley xxx

Neart chuig do chroí a Ronnie ó draoi, Rossa (Kíla)

Dear Ronnie, thanks for the music – lots of love and luck, Dee xxxx (Kíla)

Good man, Ronnie, sláinte, Barney

Lots of love, Ronnie! Eleanor McEvoy

Luv, Simon Carmody

All the best, Ronnie, love, Jack L.

For King Ronnie: respect, love and peace, Bronagh Gallagher x

To Ronnie, loads of love, Lance (Kíla)

Hi Ronnie, lots of love, from Sinéad

Conas tá, Ronnie, all good here, Grá, R6 (Kíla)

Ronnie, I hardly know you, love, Eoin Dillon (Kíla)

All the best to you, Ronnie, Larry Mullen

Ronnie Live in London late sixties just after *Top of the Pops*! Love you, Mundy

Le grá mór, Mary Black

You're fucking gorgeous, love, Mary Coughlan xx

To Ronnie, get well, Patsy Watchorn

Fada amach bábín, Brian Hogan (Kíla)

or no longer give out about you. If they're capable of recognizing that you're still alive, they just forgive, you're at the ultimate truth.

Sunday Independent, August 2007

When he gave up the drink, he met a couple of guys who were recovering alcoholics and they became friends and they worked some magic with him; he obviously saw that he had a life there and the twelve years that he was off the drink I think were his happiest. It was only towards the end of that period, when he kind of tired of the whole AA recovery process and he was getting older and enjoying the simplicity of life, that he started to convince himself again that he could have a drink. While in the last few years it never really got out of hand too much, he was back in a place where he was kind of in turmoil again.

I spoke to him a couple of times about it. I used to try and broach the subject as gently as possible, because you didn't want to take away the only thing that he had that was a means of escaping from the reality of his situation, but he actually got to the point where he couldn't drink. If he had three drinks, that would be the maximum that he could have before he would start to really feel the effects and be incapacitated, and of course it was really dangerous when he was as sick as he was.

He was kind of banking on surviving the cancer. I think that was very much part of his success in the last two years, how he survived it. There was always this deep-rooted fear of death, but at the same time there was always this hope that he would survive it.

I think the relationship that Crown [Ronnie's doctor, John Crown] had with Dad was one of 'You tell me: the option is there if you want it. You can have more treatment and obviously we can't promise anything, but it might work and it might not.' Somebody might have said, 'Look, I've had enough of a battering and I think I'll just take my chances,' but Dad was more of a mind that if the doctor thinks there's a chance and they are prepared to give it to me, then I'll take that chance.

He was never good at doing nothing. If he was supposed to be relaxing, he'd be sort of actively doing nothing. He'd be, 'Here I am now and I'm reading the paper . . . and I'm doing nothing now – just

Ronnie singing at his niece Róisín Drew's wedding in March 2008

reading the paper . . . and I'm still reading the paper.' Or he'd be doing a crossword puzzle. But there would always be a feeling of 'should be doing a gig'. Even when he was very sick, towards the end, at times because pneumonia sometimes causes people to be disorientated and have slight hallucinations. Any time he went through these little episodes he always thought he had a gig on and who was going to cover for the gig and did the lads know that he was sick and that he wouldn't be able to make the gig. It was amazing that even in that state he was always on about the gig.

The week before he went into hospital for the last time he came down the stairs and he was dressed in a suit like he always was and he had a nice shirt on and everything. And he came into the sitting room and he sat in what would have been my chair as a child; he couldn't even

Barney McKenna at Ronnie's funeral

*Shane MacGowan, with Eamonn Campbell in the background, at the
reception after Ronnie's funeral*

*Opposite page: Eleanor Shanley and Mike Hanrahan performing at the
post-funeral reception*

make it over to his own chair. Cliodhna went upstairs to get something before we left for the hospital and I just said to him do you want to come into the kitchen and have a small cup of coffee and a cigar before you go? And he just said, 'No, no. I just want to get going.' He knew that he needed to be in hospital. It was his decision and he knew that he would get the best care in there.

I was foostering about the sitting room, waiting, and he said to me, 'Oh, by the way, Joxer,' – 'cause that was my nickname, Joxer – 'by the way, Joxer, if anything happens to me, if I should go suddenly or anything like that, we're not going to the Marriott Hotel. It's too fucking expensive.' We'd gone to the Marriott for my mother and he didn't begrudge the expense, but I think what happened was that he went up to the Marriott with my sister and a friend of ours to pay the bill and they presented him with it without even asking him what he was having to drink. I think he took huge umbrage at that. Rightly so. I think these people they get a bit used to handing people bills and they sometimes forget the circumstances.

We were laughing afterwards. I was going, 'Jesus, if he knew that we had gone to the Ritz Carlton.' We stayed over there. We went back to the house in Greystones the night of my mother's funeral, and, while it was great that we were able to go back there and tell stories and share memories, it was a bit hard the next day waking up. The next day of the rest of your life.

Phelim, October 2008

PART 5

Sez He

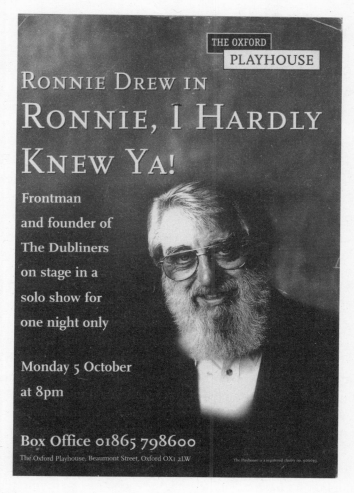

THE OXFORD
PLAYHOUSE

RONNIE DREW IN
RONNIE, I HARDLY
KNEW YA!

Frontman
and founder of
The Dubliners
on stage in a
solo show for
one night only

Monday 5 October
at 8pm

Box Office 01865 798600

The Oxford Playhouse, Beaumont Street, Oxford OX1 2LW   The Playhouse is a registered charity no. 900019.

Over the years, Ronnie Drew devised a number of one-man shows, shows that combined his love of yarns about his family and great and not-so-great Irish characters and their foibles, his devotion to writers such as Kavanagh, Behan, Joyce and O'Casey, and his passion for song – comic, satiric or tragic. He took particular pride in the show that launched his solo career in the mid-1990s, Ronnie, I Hardly Knew Ya!, *which evolved into* An Evening with Ronnie Drew. *What follows is a distillation of material from his one-man shows from four decades and includes some of the songs that meant the most to him throughout his career.*

Lord Nelson used to keep his eye on the citizens of Dublin as they walked up and down O'Connell Street. He wasn't the only one to do this, no less a personage than Queen Victoria herself did much the same thing when she came to Dublin about a hundred years ago.

Now I wasn't actually there myself, but I have this story – and I swear to you there is not a word of exaggeration in it; it's straight from the lips of an ex-Dublin Fusilier.

'I'm an ould soldier, Ronnie, me son, but do you know which soldier I am? I'm the soldier that was picked to be Queen Victoria's aide-de-camp when she come to Dublin in 1897, there's one for yeh! When she come to Dublin she was to review the troops outside of the General Post Office. There we were outside of the G.P.O. – me and the queen. Now she was sittin' down, naturally enough, on account of she was the queen. Now the first thing we heard was the drums and the bugles blowin' out.

'"Well, put it there, Paddy," sez she. Now this is the gospel truth! "Well," sez she, "may I never lift me elbow to another bottle o' stout but by Jaysus, them is troops."'

Queen Victoria's digs when she came to Dublin were at a place called the Vice-Regal Lodge, since renamed Áras an Uachtaráin in the Phoenix Park. It was here that she entertained the luminaries of Dublin society, while the lesser citizens entertained themselves around the corner at the Phoenix Park Races. Indeed, I was often there myself.

One day, after the races, I went into a pub for a drink – that's not to say that I didn't have a drink during the races. As I went into the pub, I saw standing at the counter a low-sized man in a cap. And I knew by the gimp of him, I just knew, that he was a little Dublin oul' fella, and that one of his jobs in life was being a bookie's runner.

Without looking at me, he saluted me with a 'Howr'ya, Ronnie.'

Now this is the kind of casual greeting that sends out a subtle message. It means you have been elected to ask him 'What are ya havin'?'

'Ah sure, I'll try a drop of whiskey.'

Then to take a rise out of him I said, 'That stuff'll kill you one of these days.'

He looked at the whiskey and said, 'Well, it killed me father when he was fifty-nine, but I'll tell you one thing, it won't kill me when I'm fifty-nine.'

'How do you know?'

'Because I'm sixty-nine.'

Maybe there is somethin' in whiskey after all, because he certainly didn't look it.

'But there's good things about whiskey,' he said, as he rolled it around in the glass, looking at it intently . . .

'It looks lovely . . .

'It tastes lovely . . .

'It smells lovely . . .'

He then drank it down in one go and said, 'And it doesn't kill you instantly.'

Nowadays, we Irish are delighted that we have people all over the world, mostly because it gives us an excuse to toast their success or lack of it. But we never really forget just what it was that made the coffin ships sail. And Shane MacGowan remembers the Great Famine in this song.

THE DUNES

I walked today on the cold grey shore
where I watched when I was much younger
while they built the dunes upon the sand
for the dead from the Great Hunger
for the dead from the Great Hunger.

Although I was a doctor's son
I gazed in fear and wonder
as they perished from the raging plague
that came in from the Great Hunger
that came in from the Great Hunger.

When I watched at the age of four
in Eighteen forty-seven
the mounds they built upon the shore
they seemed to come from heaven
they seemed to come from heaven.

But the wind and the rain they have worked away.
Now the dunes are all uneven
and the children kick the sand around
and the bones they are revealed then
and the bones they are revealed then.

My brothers and my sisters died.
My mother only four and twenty
and I alone survived to see
the potatoes grow in plenty
the potatoes grow in plenty.

They stole our grain as we died in pain
to put upon their tables.
The dying covered the dead with sand
and danced while they were able
and danced while they were able.

While the fiddler played we drank poitin
and ate the last of the berries.
Then knelt and said the rosary
round the mounds of dead we'd buried
round the mounds of dead we'd buried.

I saw dark shadows rise up from the sand
and dance all around the dunes
and they danced the rattling dance of the dead
to a set of mournful tunes
to a set of mournful tunes.

A crack of lightning split the sky.
The rain on the dunes it poured.
I left them lying where I shot them down
the bailiff and the landlord
then I went for a drink in Westport.

I walked today on the cold grey shore
where I watched when I was much younger
while they built the dunes upon the sand
for the dead from the Great Hunger
for the dead from the Great Hunger.

There was another oul' fella from Dublin – not that oul' fella, nor this oul' fella – but another oul' fella, and it had a go at killing him instantly. A fella by the name of Tim Finnegan.

FINNEGAN'S WAKE

Tim Finnegan lived in Walkin' Street, a gentle Irishman mighty odd
He had a brogue both rich and sweet, an' to rise in the world he carried a
    hod
You see he'd a sort of a tippler's way, but for the love for the liquor poor
    Tim was born
To help him on his way each day, he'd a drop of the craythur every morn

Whack fol the dah now, dance to yer partner, around the flure yer trotters
    shake
Wasn't it the truth I told you? Lots of fun at Finnegan's Wake

One morning Tim got rather full, his head felt heavy, which made him
    shake
Fell from a ladder and he broke his skull, and they carried him home his
    corpse to wake
Rolled him up in a nice clean sheet, and laid him out upon the bed
A bottle of whiskey at his feet and a barrel of porter at his head

Whack fol the dah now, dance to yer partner, around the flure yer trotters
    shake
Wasn't it the truth I told you? Lots of fun at Finnegan's Wake

His friends assembled at the wake, and Mrs Finnegan called for lunch
First she brought in tay and cake, then pipes, tobacco and whiskey punch
Biddy O'Brien began to cry, 'Such a nice clean corpse, did you ever see,
Tim, mavourneen, why did you die?', 'Will ye hould your gob?' said Paddy
    McGee

Whack fol the dah now, dance to yer partner, around the flure yer trotters
    shake
Wasn't it the truth I told you? Lots of fun at Finnegan's Wake

Then Maggie O'Connor took up the job. 'Biddy,' says she, 'you're wrong,
    I'm sure.'
Biddy gave her a belt in the gob and left her sprawling on the floor
Then the war did soon engage, 'twas woman to woman and man to man
Shillelagh law was all the rage and a row and a ruction soon began

Whack fol the dah now, dance to yer partner, around the flure yer trotters
    shake
Wasn't it the truth I told you? Lots of fun at Finnegan's Wake

Mickey Maloney ducked his head when a bucket of whiskey flew at him
It missed, and falling on the bed, the liquor scattered over Tim
Bedad he revives, see how he rises, Timothy rising from the bed
Saying, 'Whittle your whiskey around like blazes, t'underin' Jaysus, do ye
    think I'm dead?'

Tim was of course a builder, and we Irish are nearly as famous for
our building workers as we are for our drinkers. During the period
1939 to 1945 there was a very big war goin' on. It was called World
War Two everywhere – except of course in Ireland, where it was called
'the Emergency'. During this 'Emergency' England had suffered a lot
from air raids and all that stuff. So they sent for our fellows to come
and help to rebuild essential services, like houses, and roads and

bridges, and maybe a few pubs. And while they were there I suppose they helped to make England into a fit place for Irish people to live in. A lot of the lads went to work for a man by the name of Mr Robert McAlpine; he's now Lord McAlpine.

MCALPINE'S FUSILIERS

'Twas in the year of 'thirty-nine/When the sky was full of lead
When Hitler was heading for Poland/And Paddy, for Holyhead.
Come all you pincher laddies/And you long-distance men
Don't ever work for McAlpine/For Wimpey, or John Laing
You'll stand behind a mixer/And your skin is turned to tan
And they'll say, Good on you, Paddy/With your boat-fare in your hand
The craic was good in Cricklewood/And they wouldn't leave the Crown
With glasses flying and Biddy's crying/'Cause Paddy was going to town
Oh mother dear, I'm over here/And I'm never coming back
What keeps me here is the reek o' beer/The ladies and the craic
I come from County Kerry/The land of eggs and bacon
And if you think I'll eat your fish 'n' chips/Oh dear then you're mistaken

As down the glen came McAlpine's men/With their shovels slung behind
    them
'Twas in the pub they drank the sub/And out in the spike you'll find them
They sweated blood and they washed down mud/With pints and quarts
    of beer
And now we're on the road again/With McAlpine's fusiliers

I stripped to the skin with the Darky Finn/Way down on the Isle of Grain
With the Horseface Toole I knew the rule/No money if you stopped for
    rain
McAlpine's god is a well-filled hod/Your shoulders cut to bits and
    seared
And woe to he went to look for tea/With McAlpine's fusiliers

I remember the day that the Bear O'Shea/Fell into a concrete stairs
What the Horseface said when he saw him dead/It wasn't what the rich
    call prayers

I'm a navvy short, was the one retort/That reached unto my ears
When the going is rough you must be tough/With McAlpine's fusiliers

I've worked till the sweat it has had me beat/With Russian, Czech and
    Pole
On shuttering jams up in the hydro-dams/Or underneath the Thames in
    a hole
I've grafted hard and I've got my cards/And many a ganger's fist across
    my ears
If you pride your life don't join, by Christ!/With McAlpine's fusiliers

Of course these building workers weren't the only Irish people to emigrate; as a matter of fact there are ten times as many Irish people in America as there are in Ireland and the same probably goes for England and Australia. Now this keeps the telephone company in Ireland very happy, and I know what keeps them happy because I worked for them once. And it certainly wasn't me.

You see, as a young fella I was a terrible trial to my family. I didn't want to go to school, I had no interest in learning anything. Part of the reason for this was that I had this grandmother who kept predicting the end of the world, so I couldn't see the point in schooling if Gabriel was about to blow his trumpet. They tried to make me into a carpenter, a plumber, an electrician. Nothin' worked, including me. I ended up getting all sorts of dead-end jobs, and eventually I was signing on at the Labour Exchange, which lasted about three months, and in those days that would have been another black mark against you. They just couldn't get any good out of me. I got a job in the Telephone Exchange and the family thought I was set up for life. But that didn't work out either. So I took off to Spain with a few other so-called oddballs.

VIVA LA QUINTA BRIGADA

Around the time I saw the light of morning
A comradeship of heroes was laid
From every corner of the world came sailing
The Fifteenth International Brigade.

They came to stand beside the blazing people
To try and stem the rising fascist tide
Franco's allies were the powerful and wealthy
Frank Ryan's men came from the other side.

Even the olives were bleeding
As the battle for Madrid it thundered on
Truth and love against the force of evil
Brotherhood against the fascist clan.

Viva la Quinta Brigada,
'No Pasaran', the pledge that made them fight
'Adelante' was the cry around the hillside
Let us all remember them tonight.

Bob Hilliard was a Church of Ireland pastor
From Killarney across the Pyrenees he came
From Derry came a brave young Christian Brother
And side by side they fought and died in Spain.

Tommy Woods age seventeen died in Córdoba
With Na Fianna he learned to hold his gun
From Dublin to the Villa del Rio
He fought and died beneath the blazing sun.

Viva la Quinta Brigada,
'No Pasaran', the pledge that made them fight
'Adelante' was the cry around the hillside
Let us all remember them tonight.

Many Irishmen heard the call of Franco
Joined Hitler and Mussolini too
Propaganda from the pulpit and newspapers
Helped O'Duffy to enlist his crew.

The call came from Maynooth, 'support the fascists'
The men of cloth had failed yet again
When the Bishops blessed the Blueshirts in Dún Laoghaire
As they sailed beneath the swastika to Spain.

Viva la Quinta Brigada,
'No Pasaran', the pledge that made them fight
'Adelante' was the cry around the hillside
Let us all remember them tonight.

This song is a tribute to Frank Ryan
Kit Conway and Dinny Coady too
Peter Daly, Charlie Regan and Hugh Bonar
Though many died I can but name a few.

Danny Boyle, Blaser-Brown and Charlie Donnelly
Liam Tumilson and Jim Straney from the Falls
Jack Nalty, Tommy Patton and Frank Conroy
Jim Foley, Tony Fox and Dick O'Neill.

Viva la Quinta Brigada,
'No Pasaran', the pledge that made them fight
'Adelante' was the cry around the hillside
Let us all remember them tonight.

That was a song written by Christy Moore, and you can tell what side Christy was on and I have to say that I would be on the same side.

Brendan Behan decided to go to Spain – and you must remember this was General Franco's Spain – on his holidays one time. Now Brendan was high-spirited enough when he was working, but when he was on his holidays – well! In any case he arrived at Madrid Airport and the police had obviously been advised and were waiting for him when he went to the passport place.

'What is the purpose of your visit to Spain, Mr Behan?'
'I have come to attend General Franco's funeral.'
'But the Generalissimo is not yet dead.'
'In that case,' says Brendan, 'I'll wait.'

As you know, humour would not have been high on the list of priorities with those particular policemen; even so, they didn't shoot him on the spot, they didn't even put him in jail – they sent him back to Dublin.

I used to meet Brendan during the late fifties and early sixties when he was at the height of his fame. I knew him well enough to have a drink with, but I never really got to know him all that well. Due to the fact that we all tended to drink in the same pubs I became very friendly with his father and mother and the rest of the family. Many years ago, at twenty-five past ten in the morning, I was in a public house – it was my custom in those days to go in pubs very early – when Stephen Behan came in. He was at this time employed by the local authority, known as the 'Dublin Corporation', as a painter, and his particular job was painting the black and white poles that hold up those yellow globes, ye know those things that indicate one of them pedestrian crossings. He was dressed in his full painter's regalia – soft hat, tweed jacket, moustache, pipe and of course white overalls. He was carrying a pot of white paint in one hand and a pot of black paint in the other. As he approached the bar, I said – knowing him well of course – 'Do ye'ever do any work at all, Stephen?'

'It's very important, son,' he said . . .

(I was actually young once!)

'It's very important, son, to keep the attitude of work about ye, look like you're going somewhere, or coming from somewhere, and no one will say a word to yeh.'

Way back in the 1930s, Stephen had lived in the slums of Dublin's inner city. He liked living there. After all, he was a tradesman, in almost constant employment, and regarded by most of his neighbours as being fairly well off; and he was, by reason of his relative affluence, able to enjoy, to the full, the conviviality, and the camaraderie, of the local pubs, which were more or less the only social outlet at the time. Life continued in this pleasant vein, until one day the Dublin Corporation arrived at his door to announce that several hundred houses were being built on the outskirts of Dublin, and that these houses would be far healthier to live in than his present accommodation, and that the air would be better and so on, and that he was going to be rehoused out there. 'Out where?' said Stephen. 'Out in Crumlin,'

Stephen Behan with Deirdre, Ronnie and Ciarán Bourke (on the tin whistle) in O'Donoghue's

said the Corporation. Now Crumlin was, as far as city dwellers were concerned, down the country. 'I'm not goin' out to that place to live, it's halfway to Cork, and in any case I don't want to live in the country.'

Officialdom, as is usual, had its way in the end, and Stephen had to move into this new house in Crumlin. Now when the Corporation build houses, certain standards are laid down and must be observed: for example, all houses must be painted the same colour, and they must all have the same hall doors, and every tenant must have a front garden and a back garden, and everybody must have exactly the same amount of land, front and back.

Now this is all very well until we come to Stephen. You see, he got what was known as a corner house, and this meant that there wasn't any room behind the house for the back garden. And, as the Corporation insisted on enforcing its own rules, Stephen got the front garden and the back garden altogether in the front of the house, if you know what I mean.

He was distinctly underwhelmed by all this. Up to this stage of his life, when he had looked out of his window in Russel Street, his view was of a not very well-tended window box, and if he had reached out he could almost have touched the house across the street. He was now looking out at what to him was a vast tract of land, and he felt as if he was living out in the middle of a field. His wife, Kathleen, didn't make life any easier for him, because she kept suggesting that he might dig the garden, and plant grass and flowers, and that they could have a lovely garden like the man next door. But he just wasn't a garden diggin' kind of a man.

One evening, when Stephen came home from what he amusingly called work, he said to the wife: 'Kathleen! There's an awful smell out in the front garden.'

'I know,' she said, 'it's manure for the flowers.'

'And where did you get it?'

'I bought it off the dairyman.'

At this he became very indignant and stood up to his full height, which wasn't great, and said, 'D'ye mean to stand there, woman, and tell me that you're after landing out good drinkin' money on a load of shite?'

'Well!' said Kathleen. 'If you don't like it, why don't you bury it?'

Stephen wasn't going to be caught that handy, oh no.

So he took himself and his troubled mind off to the local pub, where he thought the matter out, over a few pints, and a few small ones.

He then remembered, having read it in one of the newspapers, that the Special Branch had just been formed, and that their headquarters were at Dublin Castle. So he went over to the telephone that was hanging on the wall in the pub – strangely enough, in the public houses of the 1930s the telephones used to work.

He picked up the phone and rang Dublin Castle. 'Hello! I'd like to speak to the Special Branch please; I have a bit of information for them.'

Well, the whole thirty of the Special Branch force were trying to jump down the phone to get the information. 'There's a fella called Stephen Behan, and he lives in Kildare Road in Crumlin, and he's in the IRA, and he has guns buried in the front garden.'

The next day twenty-nine of the Special Branch fellas arrived out to Kildare Road – they left one fella behind to mind the shop – armed with shovels and rakes and spades and picks, and the poor hoors were diggin' for about four days.

Did they find anything? No.

But Stephen said, 'Fair play to them, they're very good at diggin' gardens!'

Now the Special Branch would never have been drinking buddies of any of the Behans, though they had been known to invite Brendan to stay in one of their various establishments from time to time. He was so grateful that he wrote this song for them.

THE AULD TRIANGLE

A hungry feeling came o'er me stealing
And the mice were squealing in my prison cell
And the auld triangle went jingle jangle
All along the banks of the Royal Canal

To begin the morning, the screw was bawling
Get up, you bowsey, and clean up your cell
And the auld triangle went jingle jangle
All along the banks of the Royal Canal

Now the screw was peeping, as the lag lay sleeping,
As I lay there weeping for my girl Sal
And the auld triangle went jingle jangle
All along the banks of the Royal Canal

Up in the female prison, there are seventy-five women,
And among them I wish I did dwell
Then the auld triangle could go jingle jangle
All along the banks of the Royal Canal
All along the banks of the Royal Canal

Mountjoy! Now that was one establishment Brendan wasn't too fond of, in fact, he kicked against the establishment quite a bit. Particularly the English establishment. Though he wasn't against the English per se. It was the afternoon-tea-and-cucumber-sandwiches-on-the-lawn brigade that really annoyed him. Not that their attitudes are unique to England.

Before Brendan became famous as a writer he was a professional house painter, and for a short period he got a job with the Commissioners of Irish Lights. This was a very important body of men whose primary function was to maintain, and to keep in good repair, the lighthouses around Ireland's coast. And some of these lighthouses, the ones on land, had houses attached for the lighthouse keepers and their families and were called lighthouse stations. And it was on one of these that Brendan was employed for a short time. Brendan, when writing, was very diligent, but when real work came into play he tended to be apathetic, as a letter that I came across some time ago illustrates. This letter was written by the principal keeper, Brendan's boss.

Sir,

I have to report the painter B. Behan absent from his work all day yesterday and not returning to station until 1.25 a.m. this morning. No work has been carried out by him yesterday (Tuesday). I also have to report that his attitude here is one of careless indifference and no respect for Commissioners' property or stores. He is wilfully wasting materials, opening drums and paint tins by blows from a heavy hammer, and spilling the contents, which is now running out of the paint-store door. Drums of water-wash, opened and exposed to the weather – paintbrushes dirty and lying all round the station – no cleaning up of any mess, but he tramps through everything. His language is filthy, and he is not amenable to any law or order.

He has ruined the wall surface of one wall in No. 1 Dwelling by burning. He mixes putty, paint, etc., with his bare hands and wipes off nothing. The spare house, which was clean and ready for painters, has been turned into a filthy shambles inside a week. Empty stinking milk bottles, articles of food, coal, ashes and other debris litter the floor of the place, which is now in a scandalous condition of dirt.

I invite any official of the Irish Lights to inspect this station and verify those statements.

He is the worst specimen I have met in thirty years' service. I urge his dismissal from the job now before good material is rendered useless and the place ruined.

Your obedient Servant,

D. Blakely

Principal Keeper

Even though Brendan was a hard case, he was held in great affection. Brendan Behan loved Dublin and Dublin loved Brendan, as was proved by the many hundreds who attended his funeral.

Several years after Brendan died, I was at his father Stephen's funeral. There was a huge crowd there, and during the Mass I was standing at the back of the church – my wife went up to the front but I'm not a front-of-the-church person myself. Beside me was this little Dublin fella, Joey Betts, well known around Dublin, a little fella barely up to my shoulder, always very well turned out, hair greased back, soft hat, spoke in a very clipped accent, very precise. And like myself he was a man known to be fond of a drop.

The Funeral Mass was celebrated in a church in Crumlin. I think it's called St Agnes's Church, anyway it's the one opposite Flood's public house. It was a huge place, like Croke Park with a roof over it. I'm not sure of the exact date, but I know it was during the winter, because it was very cold. There wasn't any heating in the church, and the only evidence of anything warm in the place was the two candles burning on the altar.

The Mass hadn't long started, when suddenly I get a dig in the ribs from Joey. 'What time is it, Ronnie?'

'It's five past ten, Joey, and shut up talkin' in the chapel.'

A short time passed . . . another dig in the ribs. 'What time is it now, Ronnie?'

'It's ten past ten. Shut up.'

'What time is it now, Ronnie?'

'It's a quarter . . . listen, Joey, will you shut up and have a bit of respect, we're tryin' to bury the man dacent.'

He was suitably chastised and didn't open the mouth for a good

Ronnie's father, Paddy Drew, with the legendary Joey Betts, who featured in many of Ronnie's stories

long while. Then, by some instinct, like the swallows going back to Capistrano, he says, 'What time is it now, Ronnie?'

'It's half ten, Joey.'

'They're open!' said Joey.

'I know they're open but we can't very well walk out of the church until the ceremony is over.'

'The priest will be up there for ages writing things in books and we'll have plenty of time to slip over to Flood's for a quick one, and we'll be well back before the coffin comes out of the chapel.'

'OK, come on, quick.'

So we went over to Flood's and Joey called for two small ones and two bottles of stout. So we drank the two whiskeys closely chased by the bottles of stout.

And, as Joey drained the stout from his glass, he turned to me and said, 'Jaysus, Ronnie, I needed that. The heat of the candles in that chapel was killin' me.'

*

Just as there were would-be literary and artistic ladies and gentlemen, there were of course would-be poets, as well as the real thing. Now each of these tended to patrol his own very jealously guarded beat. And they were all past masters in the art of survival. One of these survivors – the Poet Laureate of a certain establishment – was in residence one day, and he was holding forth and nursing the 'proverbial', when right on cue enters an American gentleman. Within minutes our survivor had extracted the entire personal history of the unsuspecting visitor. So much so that the American gentleman felt obliged to ask, 'And what is it you do yourself, sir?' Poet! This astounding piece of information called for an immediate celebration. I mean it isn't every day you meet a 'real live poet'. Over the next hour or so, many mutual healths were drunk – at no little cost to the victim's generosity.

Then disaster struck! Enter an acquaintance of our survivor, who sizes up the situation, and in no time at all he too is deep in conversation with our American, who again finds himself inquiring, 'And what is it you do yourself, sir?' Poet!

The American, who could hardly believe his good fortune at meeting two poets in one day, again finds himself at the bar. In his absence the newcomer turns to our survivor and whispers: 'We have a live one here.' But our friend, the survivor, reaching into the depths of his most poetic soul, fixes the interloper in the eye and says, 'You – fuck off and find your own Yank.'

I remember one evening in O'Donoghue's, a well-known singing pub, there were three or four musicians in there doing just that. They probably weren't getting many gigs at the time, so they were just sitting there playing a few tunes, and they knew there was every chance that some of the customers might like what they were singing and playing, and so might send a few drinks their way. I mean they were all broke, they hadn't a shilling between them.

At about nine o'clock two Americans came into the bar. Now they weren't tourists, they were more like businessmen who'd just dropped in to have a few drinks. When they'd been there for a while they got into the spirit of things and sat there listenin' to the lads playing and singin' and they seemed to be really enjoying themselves, buyin' the lads a few drinks, and askin' them to sing this and that.

And did they know 'I'll Take You Home Again, Kathleen' and did they know 'Mother Machree', and of course what the lads didn't know they made up because they knew they were into a vein of free drink.

The party threatened to end when the barmen started, 'Time, gentlemen, please.'

The Americans seemed bemused, but it was explained to them that this meant no more drink would be served. The Yanks were a bit put out 'cause they wanted to keep the party goin'.

So they said to the lads: 'We have a suite in the Shelbourne Hotel.' Which was across the road from the pub and one of the poshest hotels in Dublin. 'Would you like to come to our suite and we'll finish off the evening properly?'

Now, you couldn't expect the lads, who were, to put it mildly, financially embarrassed, to turn down an invitation like that. They were a bit apprehensive on entering this posh hotel, as it wouldn't have been one of their normal ports of call.

However, when they got to the suite of their new-found friends, they relaxed, and played and sang and drank and had a great time. At about half past three in the mornin', they noticed that their two American friends were fast asleep, they not being such hardened and dedicated campaigners as our friends from O'Donoghue's.

They decided that they had had a very good night, and that they would not inconvenience their American friends but slip quietly away – which they did. But not before they had seriously inconvenienced the mini-bar!

On leaving the suite, they were congratulating themselves on having had such a great evening, and on having their pockets full of cures for the next day, when their attention turned to something else. You see! In those days guests in hotels used to leave their shoes outside their room doors to be polished in readiness for the next morning.

The boys regarded their own footwear, which was of the tennis shoe variety. These fellas did not in the ordinary course spend money on shoes or clothing because in their particular circle this would have been regarded as an extravagance. Well, as the hotel was asleep, they took their time trying on different shoes, to ensure proper quality and fit.

They crept past the night porter better shod than they had been for a long time.

He, the night porter, merely said, 'Goodnight, gentlemen – I see you have enjoyed your party.'

They weren't the only lunatics around the place – the pubs were full of them.

Seán O'Casey's world was often in a state of chassis, despite his being Ireland's leading playwright in his own lifetime. Mind you, if he were alive today he'd be laughing all the way to the bank when you consider that now his darlin' plays are famous all over the world. In one of his plays, *The Plough and the Stars*, the young hero, Jack, sings this love song to his wife Nora

NORA

Oh the violets were scenting the woods, Nora
Displaying their charm to the bee
When I first said I loved only you, Nora
And you said you loved only me

The chestnut blooms gleamed through the glade, Nora
A robin sang loud from a tree
When I first said I loved only you, Nora
And you said you loved only me

The golden-robed daffodils shone, Nora
And danced in the breeze on the Lea
When I first said I loved only you, Nora
And you said you loved only me

The trees, birds and bees sang a song, Nora
Of happier transports to be
When I first said I loved only you, Nora
And you said you loved only me

Our dreams they have never come true, Nora
Our hopes they were never to be
Since I first said I loved only you, Nora
And you said you loved only me

Seán O'Casey had a happy knack of turning the bleak face of poverty into a world inhabited by the most colourful of characters – which is no surprise, really, as that was the Dublin he lived in.

If I mention pubs too often in this, I am very sorry, but the trouble is that I go into them too often, but I remember being in John Ryan's noted establishment the Bailey in Dublin one night, and it was a cold November evening and I was sitting there, having a few drinks, and another few, and another few, and eventually John came over to me and he said, 'Ronnie, aren't you a terrible fool to be spending your money out here drinking, do you not think that it would serve you better to go home and sit down in front of a roaring wife?'
So I did.
I was on the dry for the next three months. I was still going into pubs, mind you, only this time I was listening instead of buying. And eh, this is a few years ago actually, there was a certain gentleman who refused to work in winter and still felt he was entitled to be kept in drink on certain nights of the week. So he arrived in one night, and everyone was a little bit tired of him coming in and getting drink for nothing, so he was shunned, and eventually he let a loud roar and said, 'What, am I a leper or something? Have I got to bring my bell? Sure all I want is a pint, I don't want to live with youse or anything.' So eventually somebody took pity on him and bought him a pint.
After his third pint he said, 'What do you think of a man getting a letter like this?' and he took a letter from his pocket and showed it to us. It was from a solicitor or bailiff or somebody who said that if you don't vacate your wife's house immediately, at once, you'll get six months without any further warning.
'You must have done something, Tony, you must have done something.'
'I did nothing.'
I said, 'You don't get thrown out of your wife's house for nothing.'

He said, 'I went home last Saturday, as is my custom after a hard day's drinking. I arrived home at 9.30, early you might say, for me right enough, but I'd had a lot of drink during the day, so I goes home and there is not a sinner in the place, no light in the house, of course I lost my key years ago, never needed a key, so what does I do, I breaks down the hall door, goes in, walks into the kitchen, not a bit of dinner there or anything, so, naturally enough, I breaks up the kitchen. What do I do then? I'm tired, up I goes to have a lie down, I'm in the bed having a sleep and I'm thinking before I go to sleep the priest is reading us from the altar for drinking and carrying on, it's not the drink they want to be watching, it's the playing bingo that has the country destroyed. That's where they were, her and the young one, out playing bingo.

'So around about 11.30, in the middle of the night, a nice hour of the night for a young one to be out, there's a big ra, ta, ta on the door. There they were downstairs. What's the meaning of this, Tommy? Like I was after packing her cases, you know, and putting them outside the door.

'Says she, what's the meaning of this?

'Says I, the way it is, Mary, says I, if you can't be here to get a man his dinner after a hard day's drinking, you had better find accommodation elsewhere.'

The Rotunda Hospital was once reputed to be the largest in Europe. Which it was at the time. I believe that we had to build another one, which is meant to be the largest maternity hospital in Europe, but since that we have had to build another one, which is now really the largest in Europe.

And I was in a street, Moore Street, which is quite near the Rotunda Hospital. It was a summer evening, there were not many people around. I was in a pub, Gerry Dwyer's, in fact. I was sitting there having a drink, and in Dublin pubs you have a very little small corner, which is closed off, something like a confession box, which is known as the snug, and there were two ladies in there, and I could just see into the crack of the door. One of them was a young woman of about forty and the other was a lady of indeterminate age. And the elderly lady said to the young lady, 'I believe you were in the Rotunda.' 'Oh,

I was,' said she. 'How many have you?' said she. 'Eight,' said she. 'And having no more.' 'Why?' said the old lady. 'Because the last one was like passing a bag of nails,' said she.

THE BAG OF NAILS

This world is just a bag of nails,
and they're very queer ones.
Some are flats, and some are sharps,
and some are very dear ones.
We've sprigs and spikes and sparables,
some both great and small, sir.
Some love nails with monstrous heads,
and some love none at all, sir.

A bachelor's a hobnail, and he rusts
for want of use, sir.
The misers have no nails at all,
they're all a pack of screws, sir.
My enemies will get some clouts,
where'er they chance to roam, sir.
For Irishmen, like hammers, will be
sure to drive them home, sir.

When Upper Baggot Street was a neighbourhood lived in by ordinary citizens, it was not very different to other areas of the city, in that Saturday night was a time when a lot of 'oulfellas' around the place came home in varying degrees of intoxication, from 'the few on board' to the 'palatic'.

There was one character who had a particular fondness for drink which wasn't confined to Saturday, and he did a lot of complaining to his cronies that the wife was giving him an awful life whenever he had a few drinks, which was of course a euphemism for being out of his mind.

But he was to get his comeuppance.

One Saturday night he came home more than usually the worse for wear. He was hardly in the door, when the wife was on her probably very justified attack: 'You're always the same . . . every chance you get you're down in that pub . . . you're never sober . . .'

And so on and so on.

In a vain attempt to put a stop to her onslaught, he yelled, 'I'm going to do away with meself, I'm going to throw meself into the canal.'

'Go on, why don't ya, you can throw yourself in the Liffey for all care. I'd be delighted to be shut of ya.'

The neighbours had of course been earwigging, as was their custom when a row was in progress, and he was very much aware of this. So he was left with no option but to make some sort of a stand.

'I'm off now to put an end to all this misery,' he shouted.

And he slammed the door behind him. And, as manfully as he could, staggered towards the canal bridge.

But he wasn't to throw off his persecutor so easily. The wife fell in behind him, closely followed by those neighbours hanging about, listening to the drama unfold, and they were all anxious to see the finale.

By the time he had reached his 'gallows' the crowd had significantly increased, and, having attracted such an audience, he could not now back down. So he climbed onto the parapet of the bridge, roared something and jumped. Now this man was about six foot four inches, and the minute he hit the water his first impulse was to stand up. The water in the canals, at least in Dublin, is only about four feet deep, so when he stood up, of course, the water was only up to his oxters.

The wife leant over the bridge and shouted, 'Go on, go on, I dare you.'

I suppose some Irish women have cause for complaint.

A lot of people are under the impression that a lot of Irish characters that appear in Irish writing, for example O'Casey's characters, are purely figments of their imagination, but they still exist to this day, thanks be to God.

In 1969–70 the first men landed on the moon – small step for man, giant step for mankind, an' all that stuff. This historic event was of course televised, and people spoke of little else for ages.

Joe Devine's Pub had its usual quota of regulars, who said they would remain there to view this programme of 'the fellas goin' to the moon' because it would be very interesting, and educational as well, and in any case some of them did not have a television set at home.

This was a kind of half-truth. While it was true that at that time everyone didn't have a television at home, it made little difference to these fellas, because they were all serious drinkers, and very fond of it as well, and wouldn't have been going home until closing time in any case.

Eventually the programme came on, they were all lined up along the bar and paying almost reverential attention to this historic television programme.

But after about two minutes the public house philosophy began.

'Jaysus, isn't it marvellous all the same, did y'ever think you'd live to see it, fellas goin' to the moon?'

'Goin' to the moon how are ye, the longest journey I ever made was down to County Wicklow for a day's outin'.'

'Oh! That's progress for you – progress my arse. I wish a bit of it would happen around here – fellas goin' to the moon in rockets, and I haven't even got a bike.'

And all that sort of oul' rubbish.

'Shh, shh.'

After a bit of shushing from their fellow drinkers, the programme was watched in silence for a while, until something happened, which caused the attention of the viewers of this momentous television programme to be diverted.

You see, in those days things used to happen on television sets. Wavy lines would suddenly appear, or snowy specks would go across or up and down the screen.

In this case a shape like a tennis ball bounced from left to right across the screen.

'What's that thing goin' across the television?'

'Oh, well, that'd be . . . eh . . . the eh reflection of the sun bouncin' off the lens of one of the cameras they do have in the rocket – oh, there's more up there than meets the eye, y'know.'

Or:

'They do have balloons that they throw out o' the window of the rocket, to see what way the wind does be blowin', that could be one of them.'

'It's the moon they're goin' to, not the West of Ireland, there's no wind up there in space, you gobshite.'

It continued in this nonsensical vein, until a man who had been standing at the end of the bar and who had been very quiet up to this, said sternly: 'Yez are all wonderin' what that thing like a bouncing ball on the television is, and yer all talkin' a lot of ignorant nonsense.'

The man who had spoken was Mulligan, and it was known that in an earlier life he had read a few 'good books' and was looked upon in this particular pub as something of a sage. So that when Mulligan gave tongue you paid attention.

The fellas were all askin' him: 'What is it, Peter? D'ye know what it is?'

But he had a good sense of theatre and didn't answer at once.

He waited for a little while until the publican Joe Devine asked him in an urgent tone: 'What is it, Peter?'

'I'll tell you what it is, remember that cheque you cashed for me this morning . . .'

Someone once said that the love of money was the root of all evil, but somebody else said a certain amount of it is very good for the nerves. Nowadays, almost everybody can buy what they want, provided they have the right little piece of plastic.

Before credit cards were in common use the citizens had to pay for anything they wanted in readies, especially if they had dealings with certain ladies who were selling things you couldn't buy in shops, at least not in Dublin you couldn't buy them in shops.

At that time the British judges held sway in the courts. But they were feeling very put upon because most of the people coming up before them were saying: 'I refuse to recognize the court on the grounds that this is a political offence.'

This was all very well for a while, but the judges were getting a pain in whatever judges get a pain in. It got to the stage where people accused of stealing gas meters and bicycle lamps were coming out with this rubbish about 'I refuse to recognize the court on the grounds that this is a political offence.'

Now these judges were known to have been very convivial gentlemen. Put quite simply, they were piss artists. One Monday morning, after a particularly convivial weekend, the judges arrived at the court. The chief judge was holding his head – he was dyin' – and he was muttering about how he couldn't put up with much more of this, and any more of this political offence business and he would go mad.

There was a certain lady brought before him and he said to her, 'Madam, before we commence proceedings, I would like to ask you a question.'

'What is it, your honour?'

'Do you recognize this court?'

'I do, yer honour! Every bloody one of you!'

DICEY REILLY

Poor aul' Dicey Reilly she has taken to the sup
Poor aul' Dicey Reilly she will never give it up
It's off each morning to the pub
And then she's in for another little drop
Ah, the heart of the rule is Dicey Reilly

Poor aul' Dicey Reilly she has taken to the sup
Poor aul' Dicey Reilly she will never give it up
It's off each morning to the pub
And then she's in for another little drop
Ah, the heart of the rule is Dicey Reilly

She walks along Fitzgibbon Street with an independent air
And then it's down by Summerhill and as the people stare
She says it's nearly half past one and it's time I had another
        little one
Ah, the heart of the rule is Dicey Reilly

Poor aul' Dicey Reilly she has taken to the sup
Poor aul' Dicey Reilly she will never give it up
It's off each morning to the pub
And then she's in for another little drop
Ah, the heart of the rule is Dicey Reilly

Long years ago when men were men and fancied May
    of Long
Or lovely Becky Cooper or Maggie's Mary Wong
One woman put them all to shame, just one was worthy of
    the name
And the name of that dame was Dicey Reilly

Poor aul' Dicey Reilly she has taken to the sup
Poor aul' Dicey Reilly she will never give it up
It's off each morning to the pub
And then she's in for another little drop
Ah, the heart of the rule is Dicey Reilly

But time went catching up on her like many pretty ones
It's after you along the street before you're out the door
Their balance vague, their looks all fade, but out of all that
    great brigade
Still the heart of the rule is Dicey Reilly

Poor aul' Dicey Reilly she has taken to the sup
Poor aul' Dicey Reilly she will never give it up
It's off each morning to the pub
And then she's in for another little drop
Ah, the heart of the rule is Dicey Reilly

Poor aul' Dicey Reilly she has taken to the sup
Poor aul' Dicey Reilly she will never give it up
It's off each morning to the pub
And then she's in for another little drop
Ah, the heart of the rule is Dicey Reilly

I got married in 1963, and we went to live, my wife and I – she came with me – in an area of Dublin called Upper Baggot Street. There were a lot of quare hawks living there and some of them turned out to be very famous quare hawks, as it happens, and one of them was one of Ireland's leading poets, Patrick Kavanagh. I got to know Paddy because of our comings and goings in the local pubs.

At the time he was writing a column on a now-and-again basis for a very unglossy radio and television periodical called the *RTV Guide*. It was unglossy, I suppose, because the Irish television station had only been transmitting programmes for a short while at the time.

One day I went into a pub and Paddy was there and I got chatting to him. 'I've seen you on the television a few times since it opened,' he said, 'so I'd like to write something about you in the paper.'

I was thrilled of course. Having read some of his poetry I regarded him as a fine poet and a man full of honesty and integrity. So I didn't have any problem in baring my soul to him.

'Y'know, Paddy,' I said, 'I wouldn't really be a great guitar player, a virtuoso or anything. I would use it mainly to accompany myself or to keep a bit of rhythm going behind whatever I'd be singing.' In those days singers were seriously pigeon-holed or categorized, for example, a singer was a tenor, or a baritone, or a castrato, or whatever you like. I was none of these things. So I said to Paddy, 'I wouldn't regard meself as a really proper singer. I'd have more of a storytelling kind of a voice, which I hope would suit the kind of songs that I sing.'

I was of course very anxious to read what Paddy had written about me; I could hardly wait to get me hands on a copy of the *RTV Guide*, and when I did I immediately searched for Paddy's column.

I needn't have doubted his honesty, as he turned out to be extremely honest indeed. It was headlined: 'Ronnie Drew is fooling the people, by his own admission; he can neither sing nor play the guitar.' I didn't read any more.

Paddy also wrote some fine songs. He met Luke Kelly one day and he said to him: 'Would ye not sing my song, Luke?' 'What song is that, Paddy?' 'Raglan Road.' Luke did sing the song, and I believe his is the definitive version. But it's such a good song that I'm going to sing it anyway.

ON RAGLAN ROAD

On Raglan Road on an autumn day I met her first and knew
That her dark hair would weave a snare that I might one day rue;
I saw the danger, yet I walked along the enchanted way,
And I said, let grief be a falling leaf at the dawning of the day.

On Grafton Street in November we tripped lightly along the ledge
Of the deep ravine where can be seen the worth of passion's pledge,
The Queen of Hearts still making tarts and I not making hay –
O I loved too much and by such, by such, is happiness
    thrown away.

I gave her gifts of the mind, I gave her the secret sign that's known
To the artists who have known true gods of sound and stone
And word and tint. I did not stint for I gave her poems to say
With her own name there and her own dark hair like clouds over
    fields of May.

On a quiet street where old ghosts meet I see her walking now
Away from me so hurriedly my reason must allow
That I have wooed not as I should a creature made of clay –
When the angel woos the clay he'd lose his wings at the dawn
    of day.

If you'd seen Paddy in any of his drinking haunts, you would never
have imagined that he'd be writing songs like that – you see, he was,
to put it mildly, 'eccentric'. Which was, I suppose, a cover-up for his
shyness. Though his shyness was of a strange variety.

One time a lady journalist wanted to do an interview with Paddy,
and he didn't like being interviewed. One day she came into the Bailey,
and when Paddy caught sight of her he raised his newspaper to hide
his face, but she had already copped him so she went over to where
he was sitting and pulled his paper down. 'Paddy! Are you not going
to ask me if I have a mouth on me?'

'And why should I, can't I see it swinging between your ears like a
skipping rope?'

He'd be going around the place with his shoes half off him and he'd be generally untidy and unkempt and shoutin' and spittin' and drinkin' whiskey in McDaid's.

McDaid's was frequented by literary and artistic ladies and gentlemen, and by would-be literary and artistic ladies and gentlemen as well. Paddy Kavanagh was there one day in the company of Jim Fitzgerald, who was a very respected theatre director. They were nursing two glasses of whiskey. In those days in the early sixties some of Paddy's poetry was on the syllabus of certain American universities, and quite often students from these universities came to Dublin to attend summer courses at Trinity College and those interested in Paddy's work would find out the man himself drank in McDaid's. (They often came to make a study of James Joyce as well. Joyce is considered by people all over the world to be a genius. But in Dublin we know he is a genius; otherwise we'd have to be able to discuss the finer points, which would mean we'd have to read his books.)

They would come in and say to Paddy, who was the manager and a great barman, 'Does Mr Patrick Kavanagh the poet come in here for a drink?'

Paddy would say, 'There he is over there,' and indicate Paddy.

'Hello! Mr Kavanagh, we are students from the university of wherever, and we have become very interested in your work, and it really is a great pleasure to meet a man of your sensitivity in the flesh,' and so on and so on. 'Will you have a drink with us, Mr Kavanagh?'

'I'll have a ball of malt.'

Which sounded to the American students a very poetic name for a drink. I suppose it is in a way, but it simply meant a large whiskey. I suppose that years ago someone was told that it was kind of mean to say a large whiskey, when you were asked what you were havin', so the name 'ball o' malt' was invented because it sounded a little more poetic and a little less obvious.

Well, as I said earlier Paddy and Jim Fitz were nursing their glasses of whiskey and the tide was going out fast and there was no sign of any American students who might have refilled their glasses for them. They were sitting there for a while when one of the would-be literary gentlemen of Dublin came in with the *Irish Times* (what else) under his arm.

'Gis a look at your paper,' said Paddy.

Well, he opened the paper and there was a photograph of Paddy, and underneath the photograph was written: Patrick Kavanagh, the Irish poet, has been awarded £1,600 by the British – not the Irish, mark you – the British Arts Council, which in the early sixties was a lot of money.

There was a bank a few doors down from the pub, and any few bob that Paddy got went through this bank; it was called the Royal Bank. At the same time in Ireland there was a very famous showband called the Royal Showband, so Paddy rechristened the bank.

'I'm goin' down,' said Paddy, 'to talk to the manager of the Royal Showbank and maybe I'll get a few pound on account.'

Well, he went into the manager's office and threw his evidence on his desk.

The bank manager was not impressed. 'Sorry, Paddy, there isn't any money in your account, and I mean, eh, after all, eh, we can't be handing out money to all and sundry,' and he behaved in a very bank managerial fashion.

Now Paddy was looking for a tenner to go on the piss; he wasn't looking for real money.

In any case he went back to the pub. Now Paddy wasn't the kind of man to answer sudden questions. So Jim Fitz waited for a while and eventually he said to Paddy, 'Did you get any money?'

'No!' said Paddy. 'He wouldn't give me a hapenny. Oh, a mane man.'

A little while passed and Paddy said to Jim, 'D'ye know, Jim, the manager of that Royal Showbank is a first cousin of the man that shot Michael Collins?'

'Is that a fact?' said Jim, who was amazed at this piece of intelligence.

'No,' said Paddy, 'it's not a fact. But I'm goin' to put it about the town that it is.'

Paddy was once asked how he thought he'd be remembered in a hundred years' time. This song was his answer, but in reality he knew it was exactly what people thought of him there and then.

IF EVER YOU GO TO DUBLIN TOWN

If ever you go to Dublin town
In a hundred years or so,
Inquire for me in Baggot Street
And what I was like to know.
O he was a queer one
Fol dol the di do,
He was a queer one
I tell you.

My great-grandmother knew him well,
He asked her to come and call
On him in his flat and she giggled at the thought
Of a young girl's lovely fall.
O he was dangerous
Fol dol the di do,
He was dangerous
I tell you.

On Pembroke Road look out for my ghost
Dishevelled with shoes untied,
Playing through the railings with little children
Whose children have long since died.
O he was a nice man
Fol dol the di do,
He was a nice man
I tell you.

Go into a pub and listen well
If my voice still echoes there,
Ask the men what their grandsires thought
And tell them to answer fair.
O he was eccentric
Fol dol the di do,
He was eccentric
I tell you.

He had the knack of making men feel
As small as they really were
Which meant as great as God had made them
But as males they disliked his air.
O he was a proud one
Fol dol the di do,
He was a proud one
I tell you.

If ever you go to Dublin town
In a hundred years or so,
Sniff for my personality,
Is it vanity's vapour now?
O he was a vain one
Fol dol the di do,
He was a vain one
I tell you.

I saw his name with a hundred others
In a book in the library;
It said he had never fully achieved
His potentiality.
O he was slothful
Fol dol the di do,
He was slothful
I tell you.

He knew that posterity has no use
For anything but the soul,
The lines that speak the passionate heart,
The spirit that lives alone.
O he was a lone one
Fol dol the di do
Yet he lived happily
I tell you.

The voice

There's acceptable voices for doing certain things, and with mine it
has to be very harsh. Well, it can be a gentle song but delivered
harshly, without sentiment. I couldn't sing a sentimental song to save
my life. But I don't have any time for roses in bloom under the moon
in June, so it's just as well.

Daily Telegraph, August 1998

Tim Pat Coogan: It is a long, long time ago since the days when we
all met in Teddy's Café on the seafront in Dún Laoghaire and pon-
dered on the wisdom of a group of us teenagers, which included my
brother Brian, Pat McMahon the artist, and Ronnie Drew, going off
to Spain to learn flamenco guitar, bullfighting, Spanish and to do a

little drinking and the Other Thing, not necessarily in that order. 'I don't know,' was the consensus, 'Ronnie might be able to learn the guitar all right, but he will be ruined if they ask him to sing with that terrible gravelly voice of his . . .'

Irish Press, May 1987

As with everything The Dubliners do, *Finnegan Wakes* is dominated by Ronnie Drew. It is the voice of Drew that gives The Dubliners their individuality as a group, that separates and elevates them above the other ballad groups in Ireland. That extraordinary resonant gravel voice crunches through five solos on this record, dominates the choruses, introduces with aggressive wit all the songs and even tells a funny story midway through the second half of the concert.

Irish Radio Telefís Éireann, September 1966

Luke had a far finer voice than me. Luke could have been a very good singer in any arena. In my case, I hadn't a good voice but had a certain way of putting a song across which kind of got me going but I mean there's no doubt about it that Luke had the actual musical voice.

Village, December 2006

Luke Kelly: What was the first song I heard Ronnie sing? . . . I think it was 'Van Diemen's Land' or something like that. And I was sitting there saying, 'He's getting away with murder. I can do much better than he can.'

Radio interview with Mícheál Ó Caoimh, KCR, Kilkenny, June 1980

Liam Clancy [on Ronnie's voice]: A voice that would rasp the dead.

The Dubliners in Concert, sleeve notes, 1965

Ronnie Drew's voice has to be heard to be believed, it is so gruff, black and bitter, yet always edged with irony and never monotonous

UK review of *The Dubliners in Concert* (publication unknown), Rory McEwen, 1965

Like a bulldog with a hangover.

Time, October 1967

Ronnie has a voice that's powerful, rasping, innuendo. He sings straight at his audience, teeth gleaming in his piratical black beard, joyful lechery in his pale blue eyes.

Profile of The Dubliners (UK publication – unknown), summer 1967

Ronnie Drew's voice adds such a distinctive touch to The Dubliners' songs. It's a deep, leery, beery voice, with a sort of corncrake quality. Mr Drew himself has the look of a wild Irish bandit with even wilder Irish eyes.

Croydon Advertiser, February 1968

Old gravel voice.

Evening Herald, July 1979

Con Houlihan: Ronnie Drew is singing more effectively now than when I first came to know him in O'Donoghue's almost twenty years ago. His greatest quality is honesty – false emotions will never find lodging in him. He mightn't make much of a living if he had to sing such songs as 'The Last Rose of Summer', but in his own rough field he is unchallenged.

Evening Press, 1981

Like coals crunched under a rusty door.

Irish Times, February 1984

To say the least, I didn't have much classical voice training, apart from maybe smoking a lot of cigarettes.

Hot Press, December 1986

Like gravel falling off the back of a lorry.

Irish Times, March 1987

David Norris: A gravel pit in the Dublin mountains bursting into song.

Irish Times, May 1987

Like he's just had a good gargle with a few grains of granite.

Irish Independent, November 1988

And what can be said about the gravelly voice which enunciates every word so clearly, though admittedly several octaves below the hearing range of the average human . . .

Irish Times, November 1988

We continue the way [Luke] envisaged things, by blending political commentary with humour and pure entertainment in a way that makes people want to listen. But above all else we do *sing out* and I'm really thrilled to think that The Dubliners have inspired others to break the age-old silence in similar ways. Especially if they were inspired by my voice. But then, isn't that what makes us Irish? Singing out no matter what sound we make.

Irish Times, July 1992

A voice like Tom Waits's grandfather.

Waterford Today, September 1995

BP Fallon: Luke Kelly, bless him, is justifiably lionized. But it was always Ronnie Drew who had the most distinctive voice in The Dubliners, a deep dark scraping sound, like he gargles with Brillo pads and polishes his tonsils with a rusty metal nail file.

Sunday Independent, July 1997

That dark-brown, pebble-dashed voice has grown in richness over the years.

Review of *Ronnie I Hardly Knew Ya!*, *Irish Times*, July 1997

I'm not sure sometimes whether it's a blessing or a curse, but I've been getting away with it for a very long time now and hopefully I'll continue to do so.

Press release for *Ronnie, I Hardly Knew Ya!*, July 1997

An Irish Lee Marvin.

Daily Telegraph, August 1998

A voice so deep it makes Lee Marvin sound like a castrato.

Sunday Times, June 2000

The sound of a cement mixer on a high-speed grind.

Cara, June 2002

Eleanor Shanley [on doing a show with Ronnie]: The only problem we had was trying to find a key. We'd start at the two ends of the spectrum: I'd be way up there somewhere and Ronnie way down there somewhere.

Rattlebag, RTÉ Radio 1, September 2004

Fintan O'Toole: It is, above all, his voice, that volcanic rumble from somewhere near the centre of the earth, that holds together what might otherwise have been a scattered series of reflections. The voice is in great shape: the advantage of sounding ancient when he was still in his twenties is that he still sounds the same now that he is edging into his seventies . . . The voice, sweet as paint-stripper and smooth as sandpaper, also makes nostalgia impossible. Even if he tried to be sentimental – and he doesn't – it would come out sardonic. Anyone else telling yarns about Behan and Kavanagh would almost inevitably be sucked into the swamp of rare-oul'-times Dubbalin melancholy. Drew's tone, whether singing or talking, is so drily mordant, however, that the anecdotes retain their sting.

Irish Times, March 2005

Like coarse sandpaper grating against gravel.

Irish Examiner, March 2005

[picking Tom Waits's 'Tom Traubert's Blues' as one of his favourite songs]: I probably like Tom Traubert because I've got a kind of quare voice meself.

Playing Favourites, RTÉ Radio 1, February 2007

I've heard people at parties, and I'm always amazed, they never pick a simple song to sing. They always pick something like 'New York, New York' or something that you had to be Frank Sinatra to sing . . . They pick these songs that are made to sound effortless by these great singers. But it's a bit of a trick, you'd want to be very careful, because

289

an awful lot of songs that sound very, very simple are very, very difficult to sing. Especially if you haven't done your homework.

Playing Favourites, RTÉ Radio 1, February 2007

Bono: One of the greatest ever voices on earth, not just in Ireland.

The Late Late Show, RTÉ One, February 2008

Phelim Drew [describing a fund-raiser he attended with his dad in Ballymaloe House]: He sang 'Weila Waila'. I've heard people dismiss it and even my dad would never give it a huge amount of weight. But he sang it and it was almost like I heard it for the first time because he didn't give it anything; he just sang it out. And the whole audience was in shock because it was quite an upper-crust audience and there was this entertaining show of various people's talents and then at the end my dad just came out and sang this flat song, a children's song, about infanticide which culminates in the hanging of the murderer. Great. Absolutely fantastic. He was stunning.

Arts Show, RTÉ Radio 1, May 2008

The voice of Ronnie Drew was chiselled out of some deep recesses where only old ghosts knew all the words.

Obituary, *Irish Independent*, August 2008

Keeping a promise.

I remember us strolling along
the banks of the Guadalquiver
— God, what a river! —
and you sang a ballad quietly + right,
which I thought was just great
for a guy I'd never heard sing, ever.....

The song was about this singer
who had loved a girl called Nora
(her love for him had been similar)
but something in their love fell over...
It's a sad but grand song
I've listened to again often since then.

the curious thing for me was
that that sad song was the beginning
of all the long years of your singing,
which, you told me, was your real
                              dream.
It would seem that dreams sometimes
                                    come true.
So this is from me to you, Ronnie Drew.

                    Joe Hackett

Acknowledgements

The publishers would like to thank Cliodhna Dunne and Phelim Drew for their gracious and generous cooperation in bringing their father's book to fruition. We would also like to thank Ronnie's friend and former musical partner, Mike Hanrahan, for moral and practical support right through the editorial process.

We also thank BP Fallon, Mike Hanrahan, Michael Kane, John Sheahan and Niall Toibin for their contributions. It is a tribute to the depth of their feeling for Ronnie that each was more than willing to write a piece for the book at very short notice and all expressed a desire to help further in any way possible. Though he was very busy in New York, BP Fallon was a particular source of help and encouragement.

We also got encouragement and practical assistance from the following: John Bowman, Gay Byrne, David Conachy, Joe Hackett, Ann Lehane, Barbara Lindberg, Emer O'Kelly, Lucinda O'Sullivan, Mary O'Sullivan, Harriet Roche, Willie Rooney, Fiachra Sheahan and Jonathan Williams.

All photographs and visual material sourced from the Drew family archive apart from images on the following pages: p. 94: photo courtesy Michael Kane; p. 121: photo by Tom Collins, 1967, courtesy BP Fallon; pp. 185, 198 (top), 233 (top), 241 (bottom), 242, 246, 247: photos by and copyright of Willie Rooney; pp. 214, 218, 225, 239: photos by and copyright of BP Fallon; p. 216: Photo © 2006 Barbara Lindberg; p. 228: Photo © 2004 Barbara Lindberg; p. 230: Photo © 2005 Barbara Lindberg; p. 217: photo by Tom Burke, 2006, courtesy Independent Newspapers; p. 233: photo by and courtesy of Paul Byrne.

Quoted material taken from the following sources (listed in date order): *Guardian*, Mary Kenny, March 1965; *The Dubliners in Concert*, sleeve notes, Liam Clancy, 1965; *Gaelic Weekly*, Tomás Fingallian, Nollaig, 1965; UK publication – unidentified, review of *The Dubliners in Concert*, Rory McEwen, 1965; Irish Radio Telefís Éireann, September 1966; *Evening Herald*, Joe Kennedy, April 1967; *RTÉ Guide*, Terry Wogan, April 1967; *Spotlight*, Michael Hand, April 1967; *Spotlight*, BP Fallon, May 1967; *Time*, October 1967; *Croydon Advertiser*, SG, February 1968; *Sunday Press*, William Rocke, November 1968; Sean McGowan Presents the Dubliners, UK tour programme, 1968; *Daily Telegraph*, Maurice Rosenbaum, 1968; *Financial Times*, Antony Thorncroft, 1968; *Financial Times*, Antony Thorncroft, July 1969; *The Dubliners Live at the Albert Hall*, sleeve notes, 1969; *Spotlight*, Michael Hand, 1969; *Evening Herald*, Joe Kennedy, October 1969; *Irish Independent*, Kerry McCarthy, October 1974; *Evening Press*, Frieda Kelly, November 1978; *The Dubliners Scrapbook: An Intimate Journal*, Mary Hardy, Wise Publications, London, 1978; *Evening Herald*, Thomas Myler, July 1979; *Evening Press*, Con Houlihan, July 1979; KCR, Kilkenny, Luke Kelly interview by Micheál Ó Caoimh, June 1980 – quoted in the *Dubliner Magazine*, 1996 edition (see below); Dudley Russell Presents The Dubliners, UK tour programme, March 1981; *Evening Press*, Con Houlihan, 1981; *Irish Times*, Phil Coulter, February 1984; *The Entertainer*, September 1985; *Hot Press*, Declan Lynch, December 1986; *Sunday Press*, Eanna Brophy, March 1987; *Irish Times*, March 1987; *Sunday Tribune*, BP Fallon, March 1987; *RTÉ Guide*, Myles Anthony, April 1987; *Irish Press*, Tim Pat Coogan, May 1987; *Irish Times*, Charles Hunter, May 1987; *Irish Times*, May 1988; *Evening Herald*, Bairbre Power, August 1988; *Sunday Tribune*, Deirdre Purcell, August 1988; *Sunday Tribune*, BP Fallon, October 1988; *Irish Independent*, Eddie Holt, November 1988; *Irish Times*, Fergus Brogan, November 1988; The Dubliners: 30 Years A-Greying Anniversary Tour, UK tour programme, 1992; *Hot Press*, Paul Byrne, June 1992; *Irish Times*, Joe Jackson, July 1992; *In Dublin*, Macdara Doyle, August 1992; *Irish Times*, Mic Moroney, August 1992; *Folk Roots*, Colin Irwin, March 1993; *Dubliners Magazine*, editors: Manuela Kohns & Rainer Burzler, published by the International Friends of The Dubliners, 1994–1999 (six annual editions); *Milestones*, sleeve notes, Shane MacGowan, 1995; *Waterford Today*, September 1995; *Irish Music*, Paul Byrne, October 1995; *RTÉ Guide*, Paddy Kehoe, November 1995; *Ireland Tonight*, RTÉ Radio 1, interview with Alan Corcoran, February 1997; *Ronnie, I Hardly Knew Ya!*, press release, July 1997; *Sunday Independent*, BP Fallon, July 1997; *Irish Times*, Gerry Colgan, July 1997; *Irish Music*, Fintan Deere, October 1997; *Sunday Independent*, Patricia Deevy, February 1998 (book includes unpublished material from interview transcript); *Daily Telegraph*, Neil McCormick, August 1998; *46A* magazine, John Hart, May 1998; *Scotland on Sunday*, Sue Wilson,

August 1998; *Sunday Times*, Liam Fay, June 2000; *Invisible Thread*, RTÉ Lyric FM, interview with Theo Dorgan, May 2001; *Evening Herald*, April 2002; *Seven Drunken Nights*, RTÉ Radio 1, interview with Colm Keane, March 2002; *Cara*, Maura O'Kiely, June 2002; *The Marian Finucane Show*, RTÉ Radio 1, Marian Finucane, December 2003; *Irish Echo*, Eileen Murphy, March 2004; *Sunday Independent*, Anne Harris, May 2004; *Sunday Independent*, Sarah Caden, July 2004; *Rattlebag*, RTÉ Radio 1, Myles Dungan, presenter, September 2004; *Irish Examiner*, Patrick Brennan, March 2005; *Irish Times*, Fintan O'Toole, March 2005; *Sunday Independent*, Sarah Caden, February 2005; *An Evening with Ronnie Drew*, Geneva, programme notes, April 2005; *Sunday Times*, 'Fame and Fortune' column, March 2006; *Irish Times*, Siobhán Long, April 2006; *Living It*, Adrienne Murphy, July/August 2006; *Village*, Vincent Browne, December 2006; *Sunday Independent*, Andrea Smith, November 2006; *Playing Favourites*, RTÉ Radio 1, produced by Brendan Balfe, February 2007; *The Best of Ronnie Drew*, sleeve notes, BP Fallon, 2007; *Tonight with Vincent Browne*, RTÉ Radio 1, Vincent Browne, June 2007; *Saturday Night With Miriam*, RTÉ One, Miriam O'Callaghan, July 2007; *Sunday Independent*, Aengus Fanning, August 2007; *The Late Late Show*, RTÉ One, Pat Kenny, December 2007; *Bowman Sunday Morning*, RTÉ Radio 1, John Bowman, January 2008; *The Late Late Show*, RTÉ One, Pat Kenny, February 2008; *Arts Show*, RTÉ Radio 1, Sean Rocks, presenter, May 2008; *Sunday Times*, Phelim Drew, May 2008; *September Song*, RTÉ One, directed by Sinéad O'Brien, produced by Noel Pearson, Ferndale Films, May 2008; *Irish Independent*, obituary, August 2008; *The Times*, obituary, August 2008.

We thank Christy Moore for permission to use the lyrics to 'Viva la Quinta Brigada' and Mike Hanrahan for permission to use the lyrics to 'We Had It All'. 'On Raglan Road' and 'If Ever You Go to Dublin Town' are reprinted by kind permission of the Trustees of the Estate of the late Katherine B. Kavanagh, through the Jonathan Williams Literary Agency. 'The Dunes' written by Shane MacGowan and John Wardle is used by permission, © 2003 30 Hertz Music (PRS) administered by Bug Music. All Rights Reserved. 'McAlpine's Fusiliers', written by Dominic Behan © Tiparm Music Publishing Inc./Harmony Music Limited.

A final word of thanks goes to those who helped bring the book together in a very short time-frame: Mike Nolan at Earlsfort Photo; copy-editor Donna Poppy; our colleagues in production, Keith Taylor, Helen Eka, Samantha Borland and Lisa Simmonds; and Amanda Rowland and everyone at Rowland Typesetting.